PRAISE FOR
INFLUENTIAL WOMAN

'An utterly compelling and distinctive call to arms to women everywhere. Dion writes with a tone that is at once vulnerable, authentic, assured and urgent. This book serves as a timely and timeless reminder that we all have the power, agency and responsibility to challenge the injustices of our time and pave the way for a new kind of leadership. Read and be fiercely challenged and irrevocably transformed.'

SHARON AMESU, LEADERSHIP STRATEGIST AND CHAIR, INSTITUTE OF DIRECTORS MANCHESTER

'We have never needed "womanity" more than now, and Dion Johnson clearly outlines not just the why, but the how. Her book is a clarion call to all women leaders to rise up into their power, not for domination but for the good of all. Dion's voice is wise, womanly and wholesome. The book is like breathing in fresh air and feeling enlivened by the experience. For any woman who is keeping themselves small, has lost herself in the corporate world, or feels that she is finally ready to make an impact in the world, this book is for you. I challenge you to read this book and not experience a fire deep in the pit of your stomach that you cannot help but act upon. This book will change you for the better!'

JENNY GARRETT, AWARD-WINNING EXECUTIVE COACH AND LEADERSHIP TRAINER, AND AUTHOR OF *ROCKING YOUR ROLE*

'An essential book, a clarion call to rise as women of influence and bring a difference to the fight against inequality in any shape or form. Dion's voice provides the shoulder to lean on, the ear that listens and the strength to motivate your engagement.'

SHOLA MOS-SHOGBAMIMU, LAWYER, ACTIVIST AND FOUNDER OF THE *WOMEN IN LEADERSHIP* PUBLICATION

'Dion's words are power on paper. I laughed, I cried, I felt invigorated and I felt understood. Dion's book made me delve deep within myself and equipped me with the tools to unleash the Woman Influencer within. I encourage you to read this book when you are truly ready to make that difference to your life, leadership and power to influence change.'
DENISE JOHNSON-CARR, JUSTICE OF THE PEACE AND CHARITY CEO

'I was mesmerized from beginning to end. Dion has captured the true essence of "Womanity" in the writing and study of today's modern career woman. She captured me instantly, and it really is a "can't put this down" read. You will want to go back and go back again to refresh, remind and reset your satnav for contemporary leadership, impact and success. A brilliant guide for women getting ready to change their world through their work!'
YVONNE THOMPSON CBE

'A timely, insightful and practical guide to help women step into their true power.'
DAVID R. HAMILTON PhD, KINDNESS ADVOCATE AND AUTHOR OF THE LITTLE BOOK OF KINDNESS

'This book will help women prepare to accomplish our most worthwhile work to date. It starts inside us. That's why I call this a "me-time" book. Dion Johnson's distinctly tough but caring voice will help you to "be more you."'
DENISE ROBERTS, CEO OF THE EDITOR'S CHAIR AND THE BOOK GYM

'Dion's is an important voice in reframing a much-needed conversation and the urgent need for there to be more gender balance at all leadership levels. For anyone who cares about equity and justice in the marketplace, this book is a must-read!'
MIM SENFT GBA, AAI, CWWS, CO-FOUNDER AND CEO OF GLOBAL WOMEN 4 WELLBEING (GW4W) AND CEO OF MOTIVITY PARTNERSHIPS, INC.

INFLUENTIAL
WOMAN

INFLUENTIAL WOMAN

A fresh approach to
tackling inequality and
leading change at work

DION JOHNSON
THE WOMANOLOGIST

HAY HOUSE
Carlsbad, California • New York City
London • Sydney • New Delhi

Published in the United Kingdom by:
Hay House UK Ltd, The Sixth Floor, Watson House
54 Baker Street, London W1U 7BU
Tel: +44 (0)20 3927 7290; Fax: +44 (0)20 3927 7291; www.hayhouse.co.uk

Published in the United States of America by:
Hay House Inc., PO Box 5100, Carlsbad, CA 92018-5100
Tel: (1) 760 431 7695 or (800) 654 5126
Fax: (1) 760 431 6948 or (800) 650 5115; www.hayhouse.com

Published in Australia by:
Hay House Australia Ltd, 18/36 Ralph St, Alexandria NSW 2015
Tel: (61) 2 9669 4299; Fax: (61) 2 9669 4144; www.hayhouse.com.au

Published in India by:
Hay House Publishers India, Muskaan Complex,
Plot No.3, B-2, Vasant Kunj, New Delhi 110 070
Tel: (91) 11 4176 1620; Fax: (91) 11 4176 1630; www.hayhouse.co.in

A catalogue record for this book is available from the British Library.

Tradepaper ISBN: 978-1-4019-6043-8
E-book ISBN: 978-1-78817-404-6
Audiobook ISBN: 978-1-78817-590-6

Interior images: Shutterstock

Printed in the United States of America

I dedicate this book

First...

*To the women who raised me and started me
on the way to my own womanity:
Lydia Adina Johnson, Hazel Ann Johnson, Clementina
Johnson, Ruby Jones and Reverend Enid Stewart*

Then...

*To Elsa-Grace Oyelekan, my grandbaby, who when
she came into the world brought with her a confirming
message from God: 'Dion... Raise Queens.'*

CONTENTS

A Message from the Author

Hey, Influential Woman. There's something I want to share with you right from the off, before you get into this book…

I'm a black woman in a white man's world. I'm facially disfigured in a beauty-obsessed world. I'm a Christian in a secular and religion-phobic world. For too long I believed these characteristics impeded my progress as an influencer, but I now realize it's *because* of them that I have something of value to say.

You may be black, brown or white.

You may be rich or poor.

You may be a woman of faith or an atheist.

You may be new to senior leadership or a veteran.

We may differ in a million ways, but what unifies us is the call to take our place and change our world through our work – *together*.

I've written this book using my own voice and language. I speak from my own particular worldview, and in doing so my intention is not to impose it on you but to invite new thoughts and conversations through which new impact and influence can arise. My worldview may differ from yours, but I hope that my message will *still* resonate with you and serve as a gateway to new ideas and insights of your own. So, as you read this book, I invite you to be gracious enough to look past our differences, take what you need, and leave the rest.

IT'S TIME FOR WOMEN TO BE MORE INFLUENTIAL

Do you sense the mystery of the season in which we find ourselves? Or do you perhaps sense a tangible difference in your own personal season? I imagine you're a leader, like most of the brilliant women I'm fortunate enough to call my clients, and that you can sense there's a shift wanting to happen. I sense it too, and I call it YOUnique timing.

Although I don't pretend to know the precise details of this shift that we should expect, I do know there's never been a more important time in history – or rather, HERstory – for the women who partner with men in senior leadership to rise up and take on some of the organizational, industrial and global challenges of this era. Let me tell you why I'm so *convinced* of this...

THE WOMAN PROPHECY

It was a beautiful spring day in 2013 and as I sat down at the desk in my home office, the morning sun made a beeline for my face. I took a moment to close my eyes and drink in its warmth, and then with a deep sigh, I reached for my computer. I'd been experiencing a dry season in my business – the kind that every business owner, if they care to admit it, has every now and then – and so I was unsure of the plan for the day.

Spontaneously, I found myself whispering a prayer: 'What now, God? What's my next move?' The answer came almost instantly, in what I like to call a 'divine download'. The familiar still, small voice inside me whispered, 'write to her'.

I knew immediately what that inner voice meant by 'her': the woman I'm here to serve. The successful woman; the brilliant, smart, savvy woman who's done well for herself, climbed the corporate ladder, made her way into a leadership role, got herself a seat at the table. She's undeniably impressive – a role model who's doing great work and is committed to doing greater work. But at the same time, she's struggling. This woman knows the two sides of leadership – the eternal privilege and honour of holding this position and the relentless daily challenges and pressure that go hand in hand with it.

I'm passionate about supporting her. I've been supporting women all my working life. For more than 20 years I was a midwife, serving alongside thousands of pregnant and labouring women, and to this day I still consider it one of my most special privileges and learning opportunities. To me, there's nothing quite as beautiful as witnessing the power, strength and capability of womankind – or as I like to call it, *womanity* – in pregnancy and childbirth.

Today, although I no longer deliver human babies, I still consider myself a midwife at heart – a spiritual midwife. I've found where I belong: working alongside women who are going through challenging, painful and stretching experiences; women who are conceiving and carrying dreams and visions, solutions and ideas; women who are bringing forth transformation and change.

This is the work that makes me come alive, so I found this professional drought strange; and even stranger was this inward prompting to 'write to her'. Later that morning, during my usual prayer and meditation time with God, I again heard that still, small voice and again it said, 'write to her. Prepare.' Almost simultaneously, a message to 'her' began to unfold. I reached for my pen to capture it, scribbling as fast as I could.

> *Prepare for the Suddenly! The world's cries are going unnoticed, unheard, unacknowledged. Soon the cry will become a shout and the shout a tumultuous thunder, and that's when we'll need you, Influential Woman. Not the conforming you, but the you that I [God] have created for such a time as this. Not the contrived womankind that the marketplace is demanding and crafting in its own image, but the womankind I had in mind at Creation for the love of all Creation.*

> *You cannot prepare for the storm at the time of the storm. You cannot learn to fight when you are in the ring. But a time is coming when the world will need the authentic womankind, when the world will need the authentic you and the authentic difference only you make.*

Prepare, get ready and be seated in both the boardroom and in heavenly places simultaneously. The time is coming… timing is crucial… these are unprecedented times for mankind. Prepare, Influential Woman. Prepare to show up, speak up and shake things the hell up – it's almost time and time comes Suddenly!

Receiving this message was such a moving and emotional experience for me. I sensed it was important, divine, and as it said, timely. After reading it over and over again I realized it was in fact a prophecy – one intended not just for me but for thousands, perhaps millions, of women around the world. As I continued to meditate on this 'woman prophecy' and think it through, its meaning started to unfold further. I heard God asking:

Dion, do you hear what I hear? Do you see what I see? Do you hear the cries of the people affected by poorly functioning marketplace systems? Do you see their plight? Do you know what I know – that there are new ways to do things? Do you know that I'm calling women to teach the world new ways to do business and life, new ways to be and lead and live?

THE WORK OF OUR LIVES

Since that day in 2013, I've known for certain that the marketplace system – the global arena for commercial dealings, the big shop where we buy and sell everything – isn't serving people *equally* well, and the women who lead can, must and will change it forever.

Even as I write this, seven years later, I'm moved by a strong and unshakeable conviction that it is so. Supporting women who lead is my personal ongoing mission, my life's assignment. I'm devoted to supporting the rise of the women who'll influence and impact the emergence of new systems that'll govern the marketplace and shape marketplace outcomes. From that day to this I've been preparing for the work of my life.

I've served as a strategic ally to some of the world's most incredible women leaders. My clients are CEOs, directors, strategic leads and department heads. Many are public servants, but I serve women from across the sectors; women of different colours, races, religions and creeds. As I work alongside them, I get to personally witness the *truth* about our experience as women in leadership. Leading is an incredible opportunity, but let's face it, it can be really tough to lead at a senior level and the pressure can be phenomenal.

When women approach me for support, it's usually because they're going through a painful process at work or some kind of conflict. Some are bored and waking up to a mounting dissatisfaction with their status quo – they want help in finding out what's missing and how to make it happen. Others are tired and on the verge of breakdown or burnout, or have challenging personal lives that put constraints on their professional performance.

I've stood before individuals and professional audiences locally and internationally to share what's in my heart. I've made videos, training series, masterclasses; I've been honing my skills, strengthening my gifts and acknowledging the talents that enable me to offer the exceptional support I know in my belly I was born to.

As I review this, my 'preparation phase', I realize it's brought me to a new state of readiness to support womanity as she takes her place in marketplace leadership – starting afresh and with much greater influence. It's served as the preamble to this book and to the work I'm doing now. This feels like a new beginning, and I'm ready to look you in the eye and call you and the other brilliant women like you to get ready to ascend to a whole new realm of influence, a new dimension of leadership, for such a time as this.

I'm not the only one who senses this shift: I've watched as across the globe, the focus on women in leadership has been increasing in intensity. Gender diversity has made its way onto the boardroom agenda, and women are being called to step up in the marketplace like never before. Something's irrevocably shifting for women who lead.

And still, somewhere inside of me, I hadn't been able to shake off the feeling that there's more to come – both for and from us. The feeling that all of this movement in women's leadership is just the tip of the iceberg, and that the time, timing and the times referred to in the woman prophecy are yet to come. And then, *bam* – coronavirus slapped humanity into crisis and suddenly the stage has been set for a new breed of marketplace influencer. It's time to get ready, Influential Woman!

ABOUT THIS BOOK

The book you're reading isn't the one I thought I was writing when I started out. Throughout my career, I've focused consistently on women, leadership and personal development; my own biggest challenge was making the transition from public sector leadership to entrepreneurialism. Out of my zeal for learning business, marketing, brand building and so on, came the notion that it'd be a good idea to write a book: my teachers and business mentors told me I should do it, and I agreed. I mean, how difficult could it be?

Writing a book about women, leadership and personal growth made perfect sense; however, I simply couldn't have imagined that doing so would be one of the biggest challenges of my life, not least because the manuscript appeared to have a will of its own. It was as if I'd been impregnated with a message – the trouble was, I couldn't tell what it was because it was deep within my consciousness. I realized, though, that I was being called to write it anyway, to write it blind.

As I was developing the manuscript, the issues of inequality and racism kept vying for a key thematic position, and I found that uncomfortable. I felt I was unqualified to write about inequality – after all, I'm not an academic or a social scientist. So when I realized that inequality *had* to be a central theme, I experienced a crisis of confidence. But I just couldn't make the book do what I was trying to make it do – stay focused on how women leaders can become more influential. Readers won't care about inequality, I reasoned, so I should stick to what they *do* care about – advice and tips on how to lead.

I also wrestled with my doubts about whether or not I have the right to write, about whether or not my truth will be palatable or meaningful and whether readers will think me credible enough to speak it. I was afraid of being misunderstood, without the possibility of defending myself and bringing clarity; I was fearful of being pigeonholed into the 'religious corner' instead of being seen as an influencer at the heart of corporate life, where I'm passionate about making my difference; I was afraid that speaking my truth would be tantamount to professional suicide – because I talk about Jesus and my Christ-centric worldview and these ideas are unwelcome in the world of business and enterprise.

Yet I couldn't deny what was coming through with fever-pitch insistence that it be shared. And then, when coronavirus hit us and the world was rocked in ways we've never seen, *it all made sense*. Some of us have been changed by the pandemic; others have been traumatized and will be healing and recovering for the rest of their lives; there are so many stories of loss and deeply personal grief. But from all that's unfolded I've identified two key themes that are so loud and clear for the world to see: 1) our interconnectedness and 2) inequality.

Coronavirus served as a stadium-quality spotlight to expose and confirm the gross inequality that persists across the globe, as non-white communities and the poor have been disproportionately affected by the disease and have died in far higher numbers. And then came the public murder of a black man, George Floyd, by a white police officer, a video of which went viral across all media platforms. Suddenly, inequality was mainstream news and racism had caught everyone's attention. I remember watching TV news on the morning after Floyd was killed with tears streaming down my face. I threw my hands in the air and whispered a prayer: 'Okay, God, I get it!'

WE HAVE TO CARE

With love and respect, and as humbly as I know how, my message to you in this book is that *we have to care about inequality* – beyond the way it affects us in our working lives. If we don't care about it, it's time for that to change. We cannot be indifferent to this problem. The whole point of our development as leaders is for us to evolve as change-makers, and the thing that needs changing right now, *everywhere*, is inequality.

Inequality is the supreme challenge of our century: the way things are so imbalanced between us, the false, unspoken doctrine of superiority and inferiority that makes some people valuable and others valueless. Our organizations, industries, sectors, nations – in fact, the entire planet – is an unlevel playing field that's stacked in favour of the winners and rigged unfairly against the losers, and I believe it's this way largely because of what's happening in the global marketplace.

As women leading across the sectors, across the globe, this is everything to do with us, and I say we've got to make it our business. We're being called to be the difference that makes the difference – we're being called to be the initiators, innovators and influencers of fairer and more equal marketplace systems.

So, while this book is essentially about women in leadership and influencing change in the workplace, it has a specific focus on inequality. I strongly believe that if we want to see difficult change come to pass – if we want to see the transformation of our most problematic issues and outcomes – we must start by considering and accepting their probable roots in inequality. I'm calling us to have a very different conversation about our role in tackling inequality and its role in the global marketplace. We need to talk about *why* inequality is still with us, and about *why* we're still seeing it in the workings of organizations, industries and institutions, across all sectors, and within all nations.

A Spiritual Revival in the Marketplace

In my view, inequality is a telltale sign of a faith deficit. Please note that I'm not talking about religion here. The idea that to secure our superiority, we need to make others inferior – so we can have what we need, or have more – is rooted in a lack of belief in the abundance that exists all around us. It's become necessary to demean and devalue people because there's no faith in abundance for all. It's a spiritual matter and right now, we're functioning in a way that's disconnected from this spiritual truth.

In the pages of this book, I'll show you why I think womanity is the key to unlocking this truth. I'm calling us to be the women who lead the way towards a more spiritually intelligent marketplace (whether we're religious or not). A marketplace that creates fairer results; a marketplace in which *everyone* can be well, safe and making their best and most dignified contribution. We are the natural champions for this. As women, we have a history of fighting for our own equality. We want to be treated fairly and we don't like how inequality feels. But we need to go *beyond* that fight, beyond defending only ourselves, and see to it that the impact industry is having in the world is fairer, more equal and just: *for all*.

We can't keep referring to inequality as a lofty, out-there problem. If we're truly serious about closing the inequality gap and creating fairer and more just organizations, industries and a wider world, we need to allow this issue to land directly at our own feet. It's time for us to make the fight against inequality *personal*, to examine who we are and how we can become part of the change.

We're in this together, Influential Woman. You're undeniably great to have made it this far: I salute your achievements, your progression against the odds, your wealth of experience and your marvellous accomplishments. But as this book will reveal, I believe that as women in leadership we're not yet done. We have greater capacity to influence change than we're currently expressing. There's still more for us to be, do, create, make happen and express when it comes to making marketplace outcomes more equal.

As I write, I imagine I'm talking with you, woman to woman, heart to heart. I imagine us facing together the truth that all is not well within the marketplace system that we co-lead; I imagine us owning the role we're potentially playing in the perpetuation of the problems and the promise of the better to come. More equality is better for everybody – not only those who are at the butt end of society. Inequality isn't good for anyone.

I know from personal experience that it's going to take both courage and commitment to introspection, to the process, and to the preparation that'll help us identify how we can grow as the influencers of solutions that make organizations, industries, nations and the world better, fairer and more equal for real.

I've been on an incredible journey and what I'm learning in a very personal way is that to evolve as the kind of influencer we're being called to be we need to heal the deep-seated hindrances that stunt our development as women, as leaders and as change-makers. Throughout the book, I'll share a few of my stories, and those of some of the women I've had the privilege to serve. In the second part of the book I'll share the seven habits that I've found are key to our ascension to the new heights of influence we need to achieve to lead the change we want to see in our world.

At its core, this book presents my heartfelt request for you to be intentional afresh, and actively engage with your own personal evolution as an influencer. The whole of creation is calling for and commissioning womanity to wake up, arise and birth a spiritual revival that'll shake the hell out of the marketplace, transform outcomes and improve the way that the system impacts both the people who work within it and those it serves. Throughout, you'll find advice and a framework for how we can become the influencers of the change we want to see in our world – through our positioning as leaders – all without sabotaging our health, energy, enthusiasm, ethics or self-esteem.

PART I

WOMANITY: WE WERE MADE FOR THIS

CHAPTER 1

INEQUALITY: THE PREDICAMENT OF OUR TIME

Inequality is a corrosive and divisive spirit that touches everything and affects us all. It can be found everywhere, permeating every facet of society. By inequality I mean the differences in the way people experience life in societies the world over: how some groups receive better products, services, opportunities, resources, outcomes and access than others, and the way this imbalance makes life and work harder for those on the wrong side of the inequality gap.

Inequality is often associated with injustice, by which I mean the grossly unfair and unwarranted behaviour towards, or treatment of, individuals or groups that threatens the life chances of those on the receiving end of it. Inequality is also associated with isms such as racism, sexism and ageism – those theories, constructs, practices, biases or philosophies that create prejudice and labels which suggest that some of us are superior while others are inferior, some are worthy while others are unworthy, some are valuable while others are valueless.

In some instances, inequality is obvious and blatant, but at other times it's covert and hidden. However, in *every* instance it causes hurt, pain and suffering for countless millions of people – including you and me, the people we work with and the people we serve. Inequality might seem good for business but it's detrimental to our spiritual, physical, social and emotional wellbeing.

INEQUALITY IN THE MARKETPLACE

I'm particularly keen to encourage your awareness of the ways in which inequality is cultivated via activity in the global marketplace system. Here, inequality shows up in business meetings and at the boardroom table; it's seen in pay gaps and recruitment processes; and it's apparent in policy and protocol, in workplace culture, in organizational and institutional traditions and in codes of conduct.

In fact, I'd go so far as to say that when it comes to transforming organizational, industrial, national or global outcomes, our efforts will be thwarted if consideration isn't given to tackling inequality. It's an issue that simply *must* be addressed.

As I see it, the global marketplace is made up of eight domains: business and enterprise, education, science and technology, religion, family welfare, government, the arts and leisure, and media. And while a primary aim of the marketplace is profit, that isn't supposed to be its *only* aim. I've found that it can be all too easy, in the daily business of doing business, to lose our connection with an equally important and fundamental purpose:

to meet *need*. The marketplace is where we trade what we need to be well, to be whole, to be safe and making our best contribution, living our best lives.

Whichever domain we operate within, we're all called to meet the needs of the people we serve, and no commitment to profit or personal promotion should undermine that mandate. So, how are things going in your industry? How are you and the people you lead in your organization doing when it comes to serving and meeting need? Who are the biggest beneficiaries of the way things operate in your realm? Who isn't faring so well? What needs are going unmet in the current system? Whose cries are going unheard and un-responded to? Does your business embrace diversity, and does that result in true inclusion in your corner of the global marketplace?

INEQUALITY THROUGH MY EYES

When I consider the issue of inequality I don't think about facts and figures, about metrics and reports, quotas, graphs and charts – I think about people and the way I see inequality playing out in real lives. I think about the stories: my own, those of the women I work with, and those of the people I connect with beyond work.

Inequality *hurts*. It isn't just another trending issue or a problem in the world out there: it's a problem in *my* world, in *my* life. I've come face to face with the paradox that brilliant people – truly creative, gifted and talented individuals, some of whom I care about – end up punching way below their weight somehow. They end up suffering and hurting in the way that humans suffer and hurt when they play small or don't get to fully express the greatness within in meaningful ways; they end up at the butt end of the organizational pecking order, insignificant or invisible within their industry.

I see people with such promise and potential who never quite make it or get to contribute in the way they could under the right circumstances; I see families and communities and societies that never seem to get a chance to express what they're truly made of. I'm talking about women and men alike: fathers, mothers and daughters, leaders – real people. What follows are just a few stories that come to mind.

THE MOTHERS

The woman was sitting bolt upright in the chair, looking pensive. Her coat was still buttoned up and her pretty scarf still knotted around her neck. Her fingers clutched at the handles of the handbag perched on her lap, as though she was afraid it might be snatched. She looked as if she was on a rush-hour commuter train rather than on a labour ward next to a bed where her 14-year-old daughter lay writhing in agony.

I'll tell you about that daughter later, but right now, my heart is filled with the memory of the mother and the many mothers like her I encountered as the founder and leader of a bespoke midwifery service for schoolgirls in pregnancy. I couldn't perform this role without becoming involved with my clients' parents – after all, those clients were girls as young as 12 and no older than 17. They were still at secondary school, with braces on their teeth and posters of pop idols on the walls of their half of the bedroom they shared with siblings; and hanging out in the park with their friends was more on their minds than attending antenatal classes.

Getting to know the family was an integral part of the specialist support packages we created, and I loved it. Many of the girls' mums were my own age, way too young to be grannies. My daughter was still very young at the time, and I often thought about how I'd react if someone told me I was about to become a grandmother. To be honest, I'm not sure what that news would have done to me.

Those mums let me in, behind their masks; they shared their hearts and worlds with me. We were cut from the same cloth: they were like me, and I like them. Sure, some were the stereotypical unemployed, chaotic 'benefits scroungers' the media are so keen to present to us, but much more often these were women with dreams and ambitions: smart women with the hope and determination to make a better life for their families. These were women working their fingers to the bone, just as my mother did before me, to do more than just make ends meet. They wanted to create a life with value and meaning: not a second rate or inferior life, but one that was as good as anyone else's.

My mum, like all the matriarchs in my family, worked all the hours God sent because she wanted to prove herself, defy the stereotypes, and be one of the success stories. In the days before women were allowed to open a bank account my mum wanted to have her own home. Sick of being rejected by landlords for being a black woman with a black family, she was determined to get a mortgage and buy a house – and she did it! So I've seen that kind of fight, that resilience despite the pushback, that warrioress strength.

My clients' mothers were determined not to let their family live out the predictions of the unequal society of which they were a part. They would do it through sheer hard work, forgetting their heart's desires or the luxury of authentic self-expression. Many worked jobs that were beneath them, sometimes two or three jobs back to back. They grew in grit, they did what it took, and they p-u-s-h-e-d and pressed their way through, without regard for covert philosophies about why they couldn't, shouldn't or wouldn't.

These were strong, selfless women who'd become hard as nails in order to handle the knocks of a system which, at every turn, seemed to want to push them back, down, away or under. They made sacrifices and they carried a huge weight in the name of making things better for their families. But in multiple ways I saw how that drive, that determination and that fight, required armour; it required hardness, toughness. Ultimately, it became difficult to know where the armour stopped and the women began.

I've seen that fallout in too many women's lives – professionally with my clients, within my own family, among the women in my network, and playing out in my own life. I've seen that hardness turn into family and relationship maladies, into misunderstandings, broken marriages, and the long-term separation of mothers and children; I've seen women trading tenderness for the toughness and grit required to run their homes like a machine, just to cope. The hardness is necessary for the daily grind of pushing against this hard thing called inequality.

So, as I entered the labour ward to behold mother and daughter occupying the space in that way, I understood it so well.

This mother wasn't hugging and coaxing and reassuring her girl. To the untrained eye her behaviour could have been interpreted as coldness, dispassion or lack of care. I knew it was none of these things. It wasn't that she didn't want to, it wasn't that she didn't love her girl: what kept her sat pert and stiff in that chair was the pain, the disappointment, the shame and the loss that came with the dashed hopes and the evidence of failure and 'being who they said we are'.

It was uncomfortable to watch. The chair was positioned less than a metre away from the bed yet it might as well have been a million miles, such was the chasm between the two – the child doing her best to go through labour in silence and the mother at her side fixing her gaze on the door as if dreaming of the moment she could dash away from the situation. If you looked closely at the mother, you could see in the corner of her eyes the hot moisture of tears that were forbidden to flow. I walked over to her with a smile and gave her a hug. She said she needed the loo and as she headed for the door an insolent tear, despite orders to the contrary, broke free and rolled down her cheek.

Over and over these mothers would tell me the same thing: 'I wanted more for her – I wanted better. I'm doing the best I can… But look, here she is. It's just like they said about us.' The injustice of that breaks my heart.

THE DAUGHTERS

Of course that particular young girl's unique path had led her to that hard, cold delivery bed, but in many respects she was just like the many others I'd met before her – a child with daddy abandonment issues and a mum who'd 'gone out to work'.

One afternoon as I left my office to attend a meeting I encountered Carly, a girl who would serve as a mirror to reflect the hidden impact of inequality. As I entered the car park I noticed a group of boys huddled in a pack; on approaching them, I saw a young girl caught up in their midst: they seemed to be pushing and pulling her and bouncing her from one pair of hands to the next. She looked like a lamb among a pack of wolves. Without thinking, I ran towards the girl, roaring: 'Leave her alone!' Eventually, with a little resistance and a lot of lip, the boys ran off.

'What are you doing out here with them?' I asked the girl, not even considering this might be none of my business. Carly told me the story: the boys were from her school, and 'one of them wants to be my boyfriend'. She looked really scared and overwhelmed. As we talked, she opened up, explaining that all the popular girls had boyfriends and having one meant having sex. She helped me understand that although she wanted a boyfriend, she wasn't so keen on the sex part – and as far as she was concerned one came with the other.

My mother's heart and instincts kicked in – I wanted to wrap this young girl in my arms and make her hear me. 'Listen,' I said, looking deep into her eyes, 'do you know how beautiful you are? Do you know how valuable you are? You don't have to tolerate that and you don't have to be around it. You deserve to be treated like gold because you're valuable. You can do anything you want and you don't have to do anything you *don't* want.'

As I gushed my truest convictions, I found myself wondering if Carly could hear me, if what I was saying was landing in her understanding. Then she laughed! I can still hear it now – there

I was, pouring out my heart to her and she laughed. It wasn't a *Oh, you're so funny* kind of laugh or a *Ha ha, I'm tickled pink* one, but more a kind of chuckle that said, *Huh! Chance would be a fine thing. There's no way that's happening for me. Who are you trying to kid?*

I wondered how this can happen when an individual's potential is so great. Where do these flawed messages come from? And once more came that familiar breaking of my heart. This girl has no idea how much she matters, I realized. She thinks, *This is just the way it goes for people like me.* She's learned that somewhere, and when I think about inequality, *this* is what it means to me.

Although the term 'inequality' sounds like a social, scientific, and academic concept, it's real and it powers the secret, hidden, inner world of real people. Inequality in all its forms costs us dearly; we've become so used to it that we accept it, but there's too high a price to pay and I don't want us to have to keep paying it. We need to belong; we need to feel loved, safe, well and free to express ourselves and make our most dignified contribution. *We all need this* – every one of us!

THE LEADERS

I think about a client I worked with some years ago: a high-flying, high-achieving CEO who came to me because every six weeks, almost like clockwork, she'd fall down with flu-like symptoms and be unable to get back up again. She had to take to her bed and couldn't bring herself to see anybody or do anything. This physical failing had become a major problem and this driven and successful woman wanted to resolve it.

My client and I spoke about what needed to happen, and here's what it boiled down to: she had to decide whether she was going to stop driving herself so hard that she broke down or keep driving and keep breaking down. It was a simple choice that she could see clearly with her own eyes, and yet she vehemently resisted making it.

When we talked about *why* she was so unwilling to lighten up, it turned out that my client and her family, who were French, had a need to demonstrate their superiority. Her parents didn't respect losers, she told me, and they'd be displeased if she didn't fight to be 'better' than those 'blue-blooded Brits who think they're superior to everyone else'.

Semiconsciously, this leader was caught up in a compulsion to compete in a status battle that existed only in her programmed soul. It was a one-upmanship game, a competition to see who could be the most elite, the most successful. In reality, she was the only one playing the game, but her need to drive herself had become ingrained and the notion of not doing so was incomprehensible.

This mindset of superiority wreaks havoc and wages war on our soul's peace. I wish I could say I was shocked at how powerfully this particular client embodied it, but it wouldn't be true. I've seen this unconscious drive many times, lurking behind noble intentions to 'do a good job' and 'give it my best'. Through my eyes, inequality doesn't only affect black people or women – *it affects all of us*. It's as if we've been programmed with a virus; we're all grappling with the lies that undergird inequality – the lies of superiority and inferiority, and status and dominance versus inconsequential and unimportant.

Inequality takes its toll whether you're thinking you're supposed to win and what that means for the way you show up, or thinking you're a loser and what that means for the way you show up. It's pain-ridden and it doesn't work at either end of the scale or anywhere in the middle. When I think of inequality, it's stories like these that flood my mind.

WHY DOES INEQUALITY STILL EXIST?

I confess to being more than a little ticked off that our cities and nations are still beleaguered and besieged by the intimidating giant of inequality. This giant blocks progress and it hinders the kind of transformation we really want to see – the kind that we *say* we're working towards. To me, it just doesn't make sense that despite the global investment in diversity and inclusion initiatives, the billions of dollars pumped in from the public purse, and charitable donations focused on reducing its effects, *inequality is still here*. I'm perplexed, and I ask myself over and over, how come?

- How come injustice, isms, and gross indifference feature so heavily in our societies?

- How come, at a time when we're breaking barriers and doing the impossible on so many levels, things don't seem to be changing at all for so many people?

- How come life is so unfair and so full of burdens for so many people?

- How come the rich are still getting richer and the poor poorer?

- How come our paediatric mental health services are bursting at the seams with young people and children from as young as primary-school age?

- How come there's so much war and in-fighting and out-fighting all over the planet?

- How come we give so much airtime to unimportant topics while children are killing each other on our streets?

- How come so many adults can't read, or fill out a form, or articulate their needs to the authorities positioned to help them?

- How come women and children around the world are dying in childbirth at such an astronomical rate?

- How come children are growing up without fathers?

- How come some people still live without access to clean drinking water, and poverty and hunger are so prevalent?

- How come deadly diseases are ravaging our nations, families and communities?

- How come the demand for social services is escalating so feverishly and yet the funding is decreasing so dramatically?

- How come black people are disproportionately under-represented in high-level leadership globally and disproportionately incarcerated in the world's prisons?

- How come there are so few black people in the policy-setting and culture-shaping realms of the marketplace, especially when you consider the billions spent on addressing this imbalance?

- How come US police officers can murder black people and get away with it – as though black lives don't matter?

I've spent a lot of time pondering these questions, and I don't mind confessing that I've lost sleep and wept over them, too. I'm convinced it doesn't have to be this way. I know that inequality is a politically charged issue – one that's the focus of much political finger pointing and blaming. To the left of the political spectrum are groups that claim to have the interests of the disenfranchised, excluded and marginalized at heart. Capitalism is named as the problem and there's a call for a move towards a more socialist or even communist form of government. And yet in my experience, the people who achieve success in the marketplace system tend not to be socialist in their worldview.

Capitalism is here to stay, at least for the foreseeable future, so I want to be clear that I'm not calling for it to be dismantled, and I'm certainly not suggesting that under the current system, individuals and communities do not possess the power and authority necessary to take *personal responsibility* for their own success and for the fulfilment of their aspirations. But what I *am* saying is that exercising that power and authority is so very much harder when the system communicates, both overtly and covertly, that you're inferior and that *your* life doesn't matter as much as other lives.

Can our current system be more genuinely respecting, open, hospitable and equitable for everyone, rather than unfairly closed or even hostile towards particular groups or individuals? Is it possible for our marketplace to become a more level playing field? If it is, what needs to change? How can our marketplace be transformed into a genuinely formidable force for equality and fairer outcomes? We'll explore this in the next chapter.

CHAPTER 2

THE
MARKETPLACE KING

Everywhere I go I hear the sound of noble intentions and aspirations. It's not as if anyone *wants* the marketplace or the world to be so unequal; quite the contrary, in fact. Public servants insist they're working feverishly in favour of the greater good; CEOs maintain that their organizations are hell-bent on ensuring they recruit 'the best talent', regardless of race, colour or creed; directors claim that all employees receive the same treatment and that their company's equal opportunity programmes really do work.

Managers swear they 'didn't even notice' that a team member was black, and anyway, 'colour doesn't matter'; event organizers report that they've tried everything possible to find more diverse experts to headline speaker panels; schools say that every pupil is expected to win; and, year on year, governments make solemn vows to meet the needs of the people they were elected to serve.

So, for the most part, everybody wants things to be fair, just and equal – we all care about the greater good, right? No one sees *themselves* as a source of the problem, and yet here we are. Inequality is rife in organizations, industries, communities and nations. Inequality roams free and is able to infiltrate atmospheres and impact lives. And our progress in eradicating it is frustratingly slow.

Being a midwife taught me a lot about slow progress. I attended alongside thousands of women in childbirth, and so I'm well aware that during the labour process, there's a place for shouting 'Push, push!' However, if the woman's pushing and yet the birth process isn't advancing – if there are no visible signs that the baby is shifting and descending through the birth canal – it would be negligent of the midwife to keep shouting 'Push!' It's indefensible to argue, 'I kept telling her to push – I was hoping for the best!'

When there's a failure to progress, continuing with the same approach puts the baby and the mother in very real danger. At some point, any midwife worth her salt will be triggered in her professional senses. She'll respond to the alarm in her belly telling her that something's very wrong and will ask herself: *Why aren't things moving forwards? What's happening here to cause obstruction? What do I need to do differently to relieve the obstruction and support this mother and child?*

THE TIME IS RIPE FOR A SHIFT

I think it's safe to say that when it comes to tackling inequality, we've arrived at the point where we have to admit we're not making acceptable progress. This baby isn't advancing – our attempts and intentions to reduce and annihilate the negative impacts of inequality, isms and injustice are failing to progress. People are hurting, suffering, dying, and we need to ask, 'What the heck's happening here?' Or better still, 'What more do we need to do?'

I once invested in property and over time I accrued a nice little portfolio. I had a penchant for properties that were run-down, ugly and in need of major renovation because I could see their hidden potential. One day, an estate-agent friend called to tell me about a property that was about to go on the market. I asked where it was located and immediately felt deflated when he told me: in the midst of an urban war zone, with lots of crime, violence and broken windows. I expressed my reticence and his response is etched in my mind forever: 'Dion, haven't you heard?' His salesman's swagger was tangible. 'When there's blood on the streets, you buy property!' What he meant was that when things look to be at their worst, opportunity is at its best.

That saying comes back to me now as I consider the time, timing and the times in which you and I are living and leading. It's like the opening of Charles Dickens' classic novel *The Tale of Two Cities*: 'It was the best of times, it was the worst of times, it was the age of wisdom, it was the age of foolishness, it was the epoch of belief, it was the epoch of incredulity, it was the season of light, it was the season of darkness, it was the spring of hope, it was the winter of despair.'

The combination of rapid technological innovations and social and political unrest – and the global impact of the coronavirus pandemic – is evidence enough that the world and its marketplace is on a trajectory for radical change. We can all feel it: turbulent, chaotic, in crisis, scary and shambolic are just a few of the terms the people I talk with use to describe what they've been feeling for a long time.

I don't know about you but when I watch the news I'm unsure whether to laugh or cry. It's a time of unprecedented confusion and the political landscape is being shaken to its core – in fact, it's not only governments but across the marketplace spectrum: anything that can be shaken is being shaken. We've watched as establishments that seemed indomitable crumbled and fell before our eyes.

Professional functions and roles are becoming obsolete; high streets are starting to resemble ghost towns; and disruptive technologies and new business models are being introduced into the marketplace faster than we can blink. We're in the fourth technological revolution and innovations such as artificial intelligence, quantum computing and the Internet are turning the world and its marketplace upside down.

TURNING A CRISIS INTO AN OPPORTUNITY

The rapid pace of this change is making life and leadership as we know them turbulent, confusing and intense. These are signs, even clues, about the time and season we're in. In so many ways it feels as if we're at breaking point. I heard someone say that the coronavirus lockdown was as though 'God has put us in the naughty corner and given us time to reflect on what we're all doing, how we're doing it and what needs to change to put things right.'

As my estate-agent friend predicted all those years ago, a new day has dawned, which means the old has been unsettled, de-established, rocked and dismantled.

Some of us find the intensity of the season disconcerting, but I think it's important that we stay present to the massive opportunity being presented to us at this time of great shifting. There's another side to this moment in history: we're people who can go anywhere, do anything, and make everything happen. We live in an age of limitless potential. It seems we can do whatever we set our hearts and minds to.

Much of this speed-of-light technological development offers up endless potential for enhancing our lives and that of others. We now have cars that can drive and park themselves; with 3D printing technology we can 'print' entire houses and even human body parts; Siri and Alexa are our personal 24-hour concierges; we can talk and do business from virtually anywhere in the world; almost every organ in the human body can be transplanted to cheat death and give people another chance at life after illness; and scientists have their sights set on making space travel for leisure a real possibility.

There's no doubt about it: although chaos and confusion reign, these are also glorious times. We've come a long way and have done great things! We have the capacity to lead abundant, rich, healthy, and wealthy lives. So then, what better time for marketplace leaders to seize the opportunity to do some really hard things – to call for seemingly impossible but important change around the more persistent challenges we face?

What if time were pregnant with possibility in a way we've never seen before, enabling us to tackle the biggest issues that prevail the world over. What if we could tear down inequality once and for all?! What if marketplace systems could become an indomitable force for equality and the greater good?

I've spoken to many a despondent leader who wants to be a difference-maker and a catalyst for what she sees as important change in her industry; women who voice dwindling hope that changing the system is even possible (you can read some of their stories later in this book). They say it can't be done, that inequality is so ingrained in the structure of their organization or industry that it can't change. I beg to differ: change is not just possible but imminent. My hope, faith and conviction about this is growing by the minute and it gained traction when I found a new way to think about and see the marketplace system.

Seeing the Marketplace with New Eyes

During my book-writing journey I went on a solo retreat to exhale, think and ponder. I stayed in a beautiful, quaint little cottage in the middle of nowhere and everything was just so: the thread count of the bed sheets was high and the noise level was low, with only the birds chirping in the trees around me. My thoughts became louder and clearer.

On the first night, I fell into a deep sleep mid-thought. I'd been considering inequality, realizing afresh how important it is to me, and connecting with my hot motivation to see inequality, isms and injustice torn out of the systems that govern our lives. I was prayerful about how I was going to make my deeply personal convictions about this issue make sense to readers of this book. When I awoke the following morning my thoughts were right there, waiting for me to pick them up where I'd left off.

I paced around the little cottage, talking to myself in almost a whisper, gathering my thoughts and searching for a way to write about it all. Suddenly, there it was! Heaven opened up and into my consciousness fell a simple sentence that excited me to the point of tears and made everything so much clearer. I reached for a pen to capture it: the concept that changed the way I think about what can be done to transform our most prevalent global challenges and subdue forever the giant issue of inequality: *The system is a king and the king needs a queen!*

Imagine that the global marketplace system we've been talking about – the one that currently nurtures inequality – is a *king* (we'll talk later about the role of the *queen*). This king isn't a man or a single individual; he, or rather it, is a human system – a powerful, complex, creative, culture- and public outcome-shaping system. It's a system created by humankind and made up of men and women in leadership at the highest levels as well as those all the way down the chain who are complicit in the way this sovereign system 'works' – all of us.

Those who lead in senior marketplace positions make up the head of this 'king', while everyone else finds their place in the body: they're the king's hands, feet, stomach, liver, kidney and so on. We all make up the marketplace king, and we're all complicit in how he functions. Can you picture it?

Now, what this 'marketplace king' says goes: his word is law and irrefutable and he has dominion across industries and sectors, organizations and institutions. The marketplace king affects the lives and chances of his citizens, customers, clients, service users and stakeholders, whether directly through public services or more indirectly by virtue of the fact that he employs people who, at the end of the day, are also the public.

The more I was inspired to see the marketplace system as a king, the more I became curious about what a king actually *is* and what he's supposed to *do*. Being a souled-out Jesus girl, my first stop was the Bible, and I saw with fresh eyes how, throughout its 66 books, the notion of king and kingdoms is central.

In story after story, God himself is the ultimate King, Jesus is the King of Kings and Lord of Lords and, cushioned in between, are references to many historical kings. But that was *my* world, my Christian world, and I didn't want to stop there. I wanted to know what being a king meant in the wider sense. So I read papers and listened to teachings that were suggested when I asked Google, 'What are the roles and responsibilities of a king?'

I learned about kings in the feudal system of the European Middle Ages and kings in pre-Revolutionary France, and when my belly for research was full, I sat to digest it all. I concluded that a king, generally speaking and regardless of national nuances, had a universal role and responsibilities: he was there to protect his kingdom and its citizens, to judge fairly, to decree and declare and ensure the law of the land was upheld, to distribute wealth and to take care of the poor. All pretty predictable findings, I thought.

What I didn't expect though, was a link to God. In centuries gone by in many parts of the world, it was believed that a king was divinely appointed and that he ruled in God's name. So a king was there not only to protect his kingdom but to protect it on behalf of his god; he was there not only to judge but to judge according to the laws of the prevailing deity. In this instance, a king was a spiritual position in a natural world: the king reigned on behalf of his god.

When I discovered this idea I was both excited and intrigued. Think about it, I told myself as I sat basking in the ray of sunshine streaming into that little cottage: what if our marketplace system were like a king who leads with a conscience. A spiritually intelligent king! A spiritually wise marketplace! What would this mean? What would this look like? What difference would it make to marketplace outcomes? What impact could this have on inequality in the marketplace?

I thought about who God is to me and about how I'd heard other people describe their take on Spirit. Whether we say God, He, She, It, Spirit, Universe, Supreme Intelligence, Intuition or Higher Self, what we're all talking about is the creative intelligence beyond us. The God I'd been getting to know cares about everyone and holds people in equal regard. And as far as I was concerned, any king who ruled in His image would do so too. So it made sense to me that if God is Love, if God is Just, if God is True and Righteous, then his king will be too. I whispered a prayer: 'Show me, God, help me understand.'

As I pondered all this I remembered another divine download I'd received several years previously, when that inner voice that spoke directly and deeply to my soul said: 'I'm calling you to mobilize Cyrus. The season ahead will prepare you for this call; trust me, follow me, continue in faith.' I'd felt equal parts nervous and curious about what lay ahead. I had faith and I knew I could trust my God with my life because he'd proved himself in a million ways before, but I had *no idea* who or what Cyrus was.

CYRUS: THE KING LED BY GOD

It turned out that Cyrus the Great, who ruled during the 7th–6th century BC) was a king with true care for people at the heart of his leadership strategy. Isaiah, the prophet after whom the Old Testament's Book of Isaiah is named, wrote about Cyrus in a prophecy – he actually referred to him by name – some 150 to 400 years (depending on which historian you read) before he was born.

King Cyrus is referenced prominently in the Bible and it struck me that this is done in a very surprising and unusual way. He's the only non-Jewish figure to be called God's anointed, a messiah, a saviour and liberator of the people. Cyrus didn't worship the God of Israel – history has it that he was a devout follower of the ancient Persian religion Zoroastrianism – and yet God promised to be with him, to make his name great and help him gain territory and reign over a very great domain.

History confirms that this did indeed turn out to be the case. Cyrus founded the Achaemenid Empire, centred on Persia (now Iran), which became the largest the ancient world had seen. It felt important that God was bringing King Cyrus to my attention once more, at that moment in the cottage. I thought about it deeply, and prayed and meditated for clarity about what He was actually saying to me. As I researched further, I learned that Cyrus is regarded as one of history's most merciful, benevolent and tolerant rulers.

One of the few surviving sources of information that can be dated directly to his time is the Cyrus Cylinder, an inscribed clay document that tells how the king improved the lives of the citizens in Babylonia (now part of Iraq), one of the territories he'd conquered. He'd repatriated displaced peoples and restored temples and cult sanctuaries, and although it isn't mentioned specifically in the cylinder's text, he also freed the Jews held captive in Babylonia and allowed them to return to their homeland.

Although Cyrus conquered many territories, a central tenet of his leadership was to honour and respect all the peoples within his empire. He gave his citizens the right to express themselves and to live dignified lives, a strategy that contributed to the overall wellness within his domain. He respected the customs and religions of the empire's diverse populations; no citizen was stigmatized, alienated or punished for expressing their difference. Could we learn something from this ancient king about tackling the issues we face today, specifically inequality and injustice in governance, administration and public life?

Cyrus understood the power of honouring diversity within his empire and this became a very successful model for his centralized administration, and in establishing a government that worked to the advantage and profit of its citizens. In fact, Cyrus's inclusive administration of his empire left a lasting legacy. This king had human rights, wellness and dignity at the heart of his leadership, and it was this that made him great.

When I first began learning about King Cyrus, I concluded that he was my sign to focus my work on leaders and kings of industry beyond the four walls of the church, so that's what I did. I began to talk specifically to senior leaders in my marketing and messages and to create services specifically for them. This one instruction, to 'mobilize Cyrus', charted my professional course and kept me on track for years.

People would often tell me that my particular style, story and inspiration would be great for young people, or men, or the unemployed, or this group or that. But I was able to stay on message, and as a result I learned so much about the realities of contemporary leadership. It was only more recently – in that cottage during the writing of this book – that I saw just how much the Cyrus system has to teach us and how that king's respect for people, culture and creed might be exactly what we need to draw on at this time in our history. And then I discovered the work of William Beveridge.

THE DREAM OF A LEVEL PLAYING FIELD

In 1942, at the invitation of the government, liberal reformer William Beveridge wrote a now famous report that created a blueprint for public service in Great Britain and paved the way for its modern welfare state. Beveridge was tasked with surveying health insurance, unemployment insurance, social insurance and the like, and making recommendations for improving the efficiency and profitability of industry in the wake of the Great Depression of the 1930s. The resulting 'Beveridge Report' called for a comprehensive, radically transformed system of social security.

Beveridge's central idea was to slay what he called the five 'giant evils': want, disease, squalor, ignorance and idleness. His recommendations were intended to level the playing field, and to make sure that all British citizens had an equal opportunity to thrive. His vision was for a society in which no one would suffer lack or want, and no one would have to struggle financially as a result of temporary unemployment or illness. Beveridge's ideas gave rise to what were revolutionary concepts in their day and are still unmatched elsewhere in the world: Britain's National Health Service, social security and child-benefit systems.

I'd assumed Beveridge was a socialist, but in fact, he was an insurance specialist with the economic wellbeing of his nation at heart. He believed that if government relieved citizens of the burden of healthcare and social insurance costs, they would in turn contribute towards the sustainable economic success of the nation. His proposal for free education for all, affordable, good-quality housing, healthcare and financial support for those temporarily out of work included diverse community living; he regarded community cohesion as important to the economic wellbeing of a nation.

It was so exciting to learn all this. Beveridge's noble aspirations for social security placed high standards of care and wellbeing at the centre of public life. I wondered what it would take for our king – this system we call the marketplace – to live up to ideals such as these. Surely we too can dream of a level playing field, like Beveridge, or honour each other more, like Cyrus the Great. I asked myself what it would take to restore our broken system, our ailing king. These were the aspirations that once prevailed in the UK. What's happened to them? Why aren't these ideas at the core of the way things are run today? Why do we seem to be going backwards? Why are the ideals that could powerfully benefit the greater good – such as equality, justice and fairness – so hard to sustain?

After learning about Cyrus the Great and William Beveridge, my soul was fat with inspiration and hope that our marketplace king could indeed be great; and I saw with fresh, yet compassionate eyes just how widely our king was missing the mark. The notion of the greater good seems to be absent in the way he operates.

The Mind of the Marketplace King

I hope you find it as helpful as I do to think of our marketplace system in this way – as a king with authority, a personality, a temperament and a powerful mind. To me, it makes sense because the marketplace shares some of the characteristics and responsibilities of a king in that it's sovereign, it has the final say, and it has a remit for the economic and physical health and wellbeing of society. Like a king, the marketplace sets the tone, the priorities and the parameters within which we all work, in almost all areas of life.

We're all part of the marketplace king's domain, we're all affected by the king, and we all contribute to the ongoing reign of the king. And as leaders, as Women of Influence, we're an integral part of the king's mind. The trouble is, our king isn't in his right mind. He's forgotten how to reign in his true greatness; he's disconnected his heart from the people he serves, and he's neither noble like King Cyrus nor revolutionary in his thinking about equality like Beveridge.

The marketplace king insists that he cares about the greater good, but somehow, we're just not able to manifest the greater good. The king is falling short of his divine commission, and there were four occasions when I saw this with my own eyes.

THE KING SPEAKS RHETORICALLY

One September, I was invited to an international forum organized by the United Nations Foundation and attended by representatives from all 193 UN member states. In 2015, these countries had agreed upon and pledged commitment to 17 Sustainable Development Goals (SDGs) that focus on the biggest, most challenging issues affecting nations, with targeted plans to tackle them by 2030. The initiative drives a call to action by all countries – poor, rich and middle-income – to tackle inequality, injustice and isms head on, and to promote prosperity and public wellbeing while protecting the environment.

So, you can imagine how excited I was to attend a session at the General Assembly's headquarters in New York. As a strategic contribution to achieving SDG number 5, Gender Equality, it would focus on African women and discuss the possibilities for closing the inequality gap and fast-tracking black women into the leadership roles of the future. I realized that this meeting was a big deal, and I was equal parts excited and terrified about making a contribution. I wondered how my voice and ideas would sound at this level; I wondered whether I'd get a chance to make a difference.

After arriving in New York, I got talking to people almost immediately, and it wasn't long before I'd been invited to a neat itinerary of meetings other than the one I'd planned to attend. One of these was focused on the goal of Ending Extreme Poverty.

There were about 50 representatives sat around a huge board table, mostly men but around six women too, including me. I couldn't sit at the table itself, there was no room, so I took one of the peripheral seats and settled in to observe and learn. It was sobering to hear the ensuing discussion.

There was plenty of very articulate, high-level talk about how to go about solving the problem of extreme poverty – or, more to the point, why we haven't already done so. We heard that it's not because there isn't enough money to do so – there is – and every now and then someone would make reference to how simple it would actually be to achieve this goal, 'if we could only get past these huge, apparently insurmountable obstacles'.

'Even if we want to make ending poverty a reality, we've backed ourselves into a set of perverse actions that tie our hands,' remarked one man. 'Our ability to build is limited; our entire infrastructure is flawed in this regard,' said another. 'There's an interest to do this, but there are extreme constraints,' added a third.

The sound in that room – a babble of voices using lots of very long words – accompanied by head nodding and blank, unemotional faces, turned on a familiar frustration in me. I'd heard it before and maybe you have too. It's the droning noise made by the marketplace king; it can go on for hours and by the time it stops, everything's just the same: nothing has changed. It's the kind of loud, unvoiced sentiment that's effectively saying: *Everyone knows we're working towards something that, let's face it, will never happen! But hey, let's keep talking about it and sharing our important and clever research, as we're being paid to do!*

I sat in the midst of that swanky corporate luxury wondering how the hell this discussion would translate into making things better for the poorest among us. The king *appears* to be working feverishly on the diversity and inclusion agenda, and on the fight for equality, and he *appears* to be utilizing the billions that are pumped into the idea of a more equal and fair world in which people are supported to be well, safe and able to make a dignified contribution. There's all the marketplace activity that *indicates* we want things to be equal. And then we have the *actual* outcome.

THE KING GIVES, THEN TAKES AWAY

I once read an article with the intriguing title 'Malawi Female Chief Comes To Power, Annuls Over 1,500 Child Marriages And Sends Young Girls Back To School'. It told the story of Theresa Kachindamoto, a community chief in the African state of Malawi, who stood boldly against tradition to bring an end to the practice of child marriage in her community.

Kachindamoto had been appalled that girls as young as 12 had husbands and children before they were able to complete their education, and she made it her goal to send these girls to school. She'd taken a step towards ending poverty in Malawi, where a 2017 UN report suggested that about 45 per cent of young girls are unable to remain in school past eighth grade.

At first, I was excited about this initiative and my hope was stirred. But then something began to niggle me – I wondered what would become of those girls: what awaited them in the education system of Malawi. I messaged a friend, an educator from the country, and shared with her what I was thinking. 'What are their chances when they get to school?' I asked.

I can't say I was shocked when she described a school system that's grossly under-resourced; one that spews out very inequitable, high repetition rates, has consistently low exam pass rates and a high dropout rate, especially for girls. As a result, children suffer extremely slow progression rates from lower primary to upper school, then secondary and further education, which in turn sets them up for disadvantage in the marketplace later on.

The main challenge is access: about 1 in 5 children of school-going age are out of school. Less than 10 per cent of those who start primary school go into secondary education and even fewer go to university. The quality of the education they receive, when they get it, is also of concern. Not much learning takes place in classrooms, so many who go to school don't really end up with an education.

'It's dire,' my friend told me, 'and it's been so for a long time. There aren't enough government resources to support basic services; and therein lies the problem the world over.' There it was again: that familiar feeling of snatched-away excitement – it felt as if something really important could shift for these potential leaders of tomorrow, but the raised hopes at that idea were followed by the realization that the odds were stacked against these children. It happens over and over again – discrete activities to level the playing field aren't sustainable.

THE KING IS UNRESPONSIVE TO THE CRIES

I once attended an event to celebrate social workers on World Social Work Day. I'm passionate about health and social care and so I was excited to hear the keynote presentation that promised to share the good news and best practice in one London borough's social services department.

I listened keenly as the obviously conscientious director of services shared graph after graph and painted the picture for us all to see – demands high, funds low and stable, outcomes predictable. I realized with dismay that her presentation sounded, almost word for word, like those I'd given when I was the programme director of a national initiative to impact health and social care outcomes *15 years* previously.

I was engulfed by sadness, then frustration, and then hot irritation as I realized that the only thing truly changing was increasing demand and decreasing government funds. Otherwise, the same people were being excluded from the best opportunities, despite their potential and even qualification for greatness: the sick, the mentally and emotionally unstable, the poor, illiterate, disenfranchised, marginalized, hard to reach, uneducated, and so on and so on.

After the presentation I approached the speaker, who nodded as I shared my frustration. She understood it, she said, and she felt it too, but they were doing the best they could with what they had. I couldn't help but wonder why such a powerful king would tolerate the dis-ease of so many of his citizens.

THE KING AGREES ONLY WITH HIMSELF

Almost 20 years ago, after midwifery and before business, I was a regional director in local government. Soon after I landed the job, I had a massive dose of imposter syndrome. I hated the role, and I didn't keep it a secret: I'd tell my boss regularly during our weekly catch-ups how much I feared I wasn't doing it right. Each time, she'd tell me to relax, breathe: 'You're doing great, Dion, cut yourself some slack.'

Shortly after this experience I made up my mind to cultivate self-confidence by faking it until it became real, and for a while I was doing all right. One day I was invited to speak at a Faith in the City conference, which excited me because if there's something I *do* know about, it's faith. I'd already been a Christian for quite some time and considered my work an extension of my faith.

At the event, I presented what I thought was a compelling keynote: I spoke about the real challenges facing the vulnerable families we all had an interest in serving; and about how spiritual principle had a place in secular leadership. As I was speaking three very important-looking men in suits walked into the room and stood behind the audience, arms folded, hand to chin, apparently listening intently to what I was saying and looking around the room at people's reaction.

A couple of days later I received a terse message from my boss: 'What the hell did you say at that conference, Dion?' she asked. 'We need to meet, so clear your diary: it's urgent!' In person, my boss spelled it out for me: 'they' were not happy with me. 'They' were bigwigs from the mayor's office, and 'they' didn't like what they'd heard me say at the conference. I'd sounded too much like 'church' and I'd crossed some kind of line.

My boss told me I was being watched; that, in fact, there were concerns about my work and I needed to 'be very careful'. She'd been instructed to keep a close eye on me and to report to 'them' on my progress (or lack of it). 'What?' I exclaimed. 'I've been telling you about my performance concerns and each time you've reassured me. Now you're telling me there's a problem? And how was I *supposed* to sound at a conference about faith in social action? How could I do it *without* mentioning God and my faith?'

I felt frustrated, but most of all I was scared. I could feel the weight of the system coming against me. I felt small in relation to the clout of the king. It felt as if the king had welcomed me to be a part of him and had recognized that he needed my input, but in reality he only wanted to hear me if I spoke just as he did. He wore a professional mask that smiled and said that people like me matter and that we're equal, while in a trillion ways equality, fairness and justice were being continually undermined.

The king let me know, in no uncertain terms, that if I was going to make it around here, I'd need to leave 'me' at the door and act like him – that being like him was 'professional', while being like me was unacceptable. So my voice went completely unheard and nothing changed – and the king was okay with that. Ever since, it has felt to me as if the king agrees only with himself and is closed to diverse counsel.

THE KING NEEDS A CHANGE OF HEART

I have to admit that my relationship with the marketplace king is evolving. I've seen, even throughout the process of writing this book, that I've viewed him with a sense of resentment. I've been hurt by him, and in my thinking I've believed he means me no good. I've felt held back and oppressed by the king.

But as I mature, evolve and step into my power, my heart is opening to the king. I understand him better, in new ways – I understand that he's concerned only with expressing power: he wants to express himself as powerfully productive, powerfully profitable and in command of a powerful, competitive advantage. He's determined to win and this is the only way he knows how.

That's the problem: the king perceives that in order for him to win there must be losers. He must be closed to outside influences because it's erroneous to believe that you can truly win while being open to them. Being aloof, numb and indifferent to his impact on other people's wellbeing is the way he is able to succeed.

However, the way the king thinks is historical; it's been learned over centuries and I've seen how difficult it is for him to see or accept the error of his ways. In fact I've seen him go to war in defence of them. I've personally witnessed him lie, cheat, sweep things under the rug, play ignorant and try all manner of other tactics to cover up his folly, to hold on to his upper hand and maintain, at least in his own eyes, his sense of power.

The king needs a change of heart.

He needs help to know that there are other ways to win.

And that he can be powerful and loving, victorious and supportive.

That he can be seen and share the spotlight.

That he can be heard and consult with diverse voices.

People don't have to suffer for the king to prosper.

We don't need inequality.

It actually serves the king when we can *all* express our true greatness.

This is what the king doesn't believe and hasn't known.

This is what the king couldn't know as he deprioritizes his moral and spiritual responsibility to care.

This is what the king must know now for things to change within his realm and reign.

His heart needs to be revived.

His passion and compassion need to heal and be restored.

And, according to the woman prophecy, it's we women in leadership who must prepare to answer the call and lead this divine work at such a time as this!

CHAPTER 3

WOMANITY IN MARKETPLACE LEADERSHIP

We've finally made it – women are big news in the marketplace, the topic of the season. Buzzwords such as 'women in leadership', gender diversity and inclusion are quite rightly on every business agenda: women are now a permanent feature of the global leadership scene. Sometimes I have to remind myself that less than 100 years ago, and in some parts of the world less than 80 years ago, women didn't go into marketplace leadership. The world of work, once virtually void of female employees, has transitioned to a place where women are appointed to the highest offices across all sectors.

All this said, we're still the new kids on the block. At the time of writing, there are only 14 women serving as heads of state, and according to Grant Thornton International Ltd's annual Women in Business Report, women held only 24 per cent of senior roles across the world in 2018.[1] Our ascent to senior leadership roles is admittedly slow, but although we're still few and far between, we *are* in!

I wish I could tell you that my own leadership ascent was a confident, bold and strategic strut straight to the boardroom. Alas, it was a far cry from that. It took me a long time to make the leap from senior management of the midwifery team I'd pioneered into health and social care senior leadership. I'd wanted to move on from midwifery for years before I summoned the courage to do so. I spent a while sidestepping – you know, when you want to change your job but aren't quite courageous enough to go for the promotion.

Perhaps your ascent was more elegant or strategic than mine. I've met women who tell how they literally fell into their role through a series of random events; others say that from the time they were knee-high to a grasshopper they knew that *nothing* could stop them from boardroom domination. We women have climbed and pushed and pressed our way in and up; we've fought for access and equality, and we've played the game to get where we are. And, by and large, we're doing well.

For decades, study after study has found that companies that have more women on their board and leading their teams benefit in myriad ways. Better problem solving, higher levels of trust and commitment to company values, greater collaboration,

---

1 Grant Thornton International Ltd (March 2018), 'Women in business: beyond policy to progress.' www.grantthornton.global/globalassets/1.-member-firms/ global/insights/women-in-business/women-in-business-2018-key-global- findings.pdf [accessed 3 September 2020]

increased productivity and of course a better bottom line are just some of what the evidence suggests women bring into our sphere of influence.

WOMEN ARE IN, BUT NOT INFLUENCING

So, however *you* got into leadership, a pat on the back is in order. You and women like you do indeed have much to celebrate: in the history of the marketplace, we've never had greater access than we do today. The workplace needs Women of Influence. We're good for business. As the science shows, we're an undeniably valuable presence in the marketplace.

And yet we must continue to be intentional about establishing ourselves because, alongside our successes, there's another story playing out too: a flip side. Leadership is hard work. The women behind the job titles are under incredible pressure and it's taking its toll on our leadership and lives.

In 2009, the Dalai Lama boldly prophesied that 'the world will be saved by the Western Woman'. As I ponder on our privileged positioning in leadership, I agree with him wholeheartedly – after all, we're in the room now, at the table, part of the high-level conversations, and this really does give us the opportunity to be the influencers of a more equal and just system. I'm fully persuaded that we women – not just Western women but all the women in marketplace leadership around the globe – represent a great hope in the mission for local and global change.

And yet I continue to meet woman after woman who, just as I did in my director's position, struggles to believe fully, or at all, in her power to initiate, innovate and influence the marketplace king. Instead, so many of us are feeling pressured by the very system we're being called to transform.

Do you own that power to influence the marketplace king? Do you know you have it? Do you understand it and know how to use it? These are important questions for us to ask (and answer) if we're to succeed as influential change-makers in our roles. So often I find that although we're in leadership positions, we're not influencing the kind of change we truly want to see in our world. We're in but we're not influencing as much as we could. And there's one thing that's severely undermining our capacity for real, lasting influence – pressure.

LEADERSHIP PRESSURE: IT'S REAL

What do we mean when we talk about 'being under pressure'? Dictionary definitions of the word pressure tell us it's the result of 'continuous physical force exerted on or against an object by something in contact with it'; the 'use of persuasion or intimidation to make someone do something'; and how much 'something is pushing on something else'. Pressure can be physical or mental and it's associated with words such as burden, force, press, push, compression, crushing, heaviness, stress, tension, squeeze, load and thrust.

THREE SOURCES OF PRESSURE

I don't know about you, but just *thinking* these words evokes a visceral response in me – a tangible sense of what it means to be 'under pressure'. Usually, it's this pressure that compels the women who become my clients to seek me out as their strategic ally. Senior leadership pressure is *real!* These leaders – those whom I coach and those who attend my events, read my content or come to hear me speak – are almost always experiencing some form of pressure. Although every woman tells her own unique story, I've noticed three common sources of the pressure she describes.

1: THE ERA IN WHICH WE LEAD

You don't have to be a politics or current-affairs buff to know that something's up. These are strange times: volatile, uncertain, complex and ambiguous. It's a season of severe socio-economic, spiritual and emotional unrest the world over, and yet here we are, in the midst of it all, leading. The women I speak with can *feel* it, and so can I. All this is being impacted by, and having an undeniable impact on, marketplace activity and therefore on us as marketplace leaders. Wherever you lead within the marketplace, you'll no doubt be experiencing the squeeze and the press.

We're all being impacted by the sheer speed of turbulent change, political mayhem, advancing technology, increasing violence and social unrest, health epidemics, economic instability, increasing life expectancy, shifts in consumer buying power, wars and terrorist attacks and changing work patterns, to name just a few signs of the times. The pressure is mounting and the women I work with and speak to express no uncertainty about how 'heavy' things are getting.

As I speak with my clients, I hear consistently that along with these external pressures come relentlessly increasing demands on leadership teams to pivot, perform, adapt, change shape and fight for custom, just to keep up and stay afloat. Things feel unstable and uncertain in business and leaders are constantly being asked to do more with less. They're expected to cope with a changing workforce and navigate customer and client demands that escalate in unison with unreasonable expectations to do the impossible.

I'm told over and over by clients, particularly those in public service and charity sectors, that 'this isn't the job I signed up for!' And as the time and season become more volatile, uncertain, complex and ambiguous, the stressful pressure leaders are under increases. How would *you* describe the time and season we're living in today? How does this put pressure on you and the leadership teams in your organization, industry and field?

2: CONTEMPORARY POWER STRUCTURES

Today's leadership power structures are a prolific breeding ground for power struggles, prejudice, pushbacks and pressure in all its forms. The evidence presents itself daily, while study after study suggests that the path to leadership and the experience within contemporary power structures are distinctly more pressure-ful for women than for men. Prevailing organizational structures and hierarchies are a challenge, and women face daily offences and micro-aggressions in multiple ways.

The Communications War

On their path to leadership, some women struggle to get a word in edgeways while others tell of how they need to pussyfoot, walk on eggshells and 'go lightly' to avoid being labelled a 'ball-breaker', a 'troublemaker' or an 'angry, bitchy woman'.

The pressure to choose our words and overly manage our body language is energetically expensive and draining. One of my clients, a COO in a prestigious law firm, said of one male direct report: 'He challenges every damn thing and usually gets his own way! I feel as if I need to constantly brownnose him to get anything accomplished, and I can't stand it. I find myself smiling and nodding and altering my voice just so he doesn't think I'm patronizing him – because then we *really* won't get anywhere. It makes me feel inauthentic and degraded!' I can still almost feel the heat of her frustration.

I recently hosted a round-table forum at which a director-level leader in the National Health Service spoke passionately about favouritism and how she saw and experienced blatant unfairness in the allocation of projects and assignments. She told the group that she often felt she 'drew the short straw' and was 'deliberately set up to fail' in a way that other white leaders at this level were not.

My experience shows this unfairness is frequently compounded and complicated when race and faith or physical differences are thrown into the mix. I can tell you that any black woman whose parents were intent on grooming her for leadership is familiar with a particular instruction, usually delivered with an index finger wagging profusely: 'If you're going to make it in this world and be taken seriously, you have to be 10 times better than other people.' And as I know from personal experience, the burden that comes with this truth can be draining.

The Absence of Allies

Many women in leadership roles experience isolation and loneliness: they feel they have no one they can trust or to help with problems and career progression. Frequently I hear women cry: 'The men have their boys' network but women have to go it alone and carry the weight by themselves.'

It's as if we're crabs in a bucket. Fishermen place live crabs in a bucket without a lid because they know that when one crab tries to climb out of the bucket, another crab, hot on its heels, will drag it back down in an attempt to win an advantage in its own attempts to make it to the rim. I've often heard women say: 'The women at the top are worse than the men! They make life harder for the other women, not easier!'

All too commonly women who lead struggle to find high-level sponsorship and allies with whom they can be open, honest and vulnerable – people who can and actually will help them. Often clients tell me they don't know whom they can trust and that it simply isn't safe to let anyone from within the organization 'in'. Remember, the name of the game is showing how capable you are and fighting for status, so the last thing you want is to raise or confirm any suspicions that you aren't coping!

This heavy emphasis on minding your p's and q's, striving to ensure you don't slip up or do anything that'll prove what they already think – that you're not up to the job – is beyond stressful for so many. It's a huge source of the pressure women are under in contemporary leadership power structures. But there's something else too.

Work-Life Balance and Gender

In his article 'Work-life balance and double standards for female CEOs', Didier Elzinga, founder and CEO of the company Culture Amp, writes: 'Every female CEO gets asked if they can have it all; I'm never asked that. Every time my wife travels overseas, she gets asked who looks after the kids. I've never once been asked that question.'[2]

The truth is that women are still expected to 'do it all', or at least most of it: the housework, sorting out the kids, looking after the ageing parents, ironing the shirts, and so on. Admittedly, the needle is shifting on this, and many men are now eligible for paternity leave, but despite the amendment of laws and policies to include men in flexible working initiatives, women still bear the brunt of managing the home while men get promoted and do what it takes to hold down senior positions. So many women in leadership are spread too thinly and spinning far too many plates, and whether we know it or not, like it or not, we're feeling the pressure.

3: PRESSURE FROM WITHIN

Of the three pressures, this is the one that I love thinking and talking about the most. I see it, I hear it, and I'm experiencing it myself. Womanity, it seems to me, is being awakened to a profound, visceral, uninvited, status-quo – threatening, inward knowing that there's more for us to be, do, say, create, express and make happen in our world. It's as if the lights have been switched on to give way to revelation; it's like a mum waking her child

---

2 Elzinga, D., 'Work-life balance and double standards for female CEOs.' www.cultureamp.com/blog/thoughts-on-work-life-balance [Accessed 1 June 2020]

for school but the child wants to stay in bed for at least another hour – no matter how much her child objects, the mother won't be fobbed off or ignored.

I'll never forget the day I met Juliette. She approached me after I'd spoken at an event for women in leadership about strategies for upping influence and impact. I didn't know how to take her at first – she seemed angry or frustrated about something and I wondered if I'd said something during my talk to offend her. I shifted myself to come alongside her in a bid to forge conditions for rapport.

With a deadpan expression, Juliette said: 'I'm one of those women you've been speaking about in your talk today!' She explained how for the last six years she'd known that being a successful lawyer wasn't enough. Something in her heart was telling her she wasn't done – that it was time for her to grow, move. 'I'm being called to do more,' she confessed, looking as if she didn't know whether to laugh or cry.

The reason I remember Juliette so vividly was the slightly eccentric and very energetic way she expressed disapproval that this was happening to her. She'd worked hard to get where she was, and she felt pretty comfortable. She could do the job with her eyes closed, and here I was, 'colluding with God', as she put it, to poke and provoke her into 'getting the message' when all she'd wanted was an informative and engaging evening of networking with her friend and colleague.

We spoke for a while that evening. Eventually Juliette cracked a smile and before long, she let her raucous laughter rip; she was actually a really funny woman. But behind the smiles I knew that what she was expressing was something I've experienced myself and seen time and again: *the pressure from within.*

I'm personally aware of hundreds, and know there are perhaps millions, of women around the globe who are waking up to a very personal inner pressure – maybe you feel it too. I also think we hold a collective realization that it's time to be more than we're being: to make more difference, to experience something new. We're becoming present to a sense of calling and a compelling conviction that we're not done, that there's more in store than what we've achieved.

Some women experience it as a vague hunch; others are forcefully pressed from their inner world. Juliette isn't the only woman I've heard describe this uninvited nudge as unwelcome and inconvenient; for many, this mounting 'push for more' seems uncomfortable and a threat to their comfort zone. For some women, it's actually frightening because it's not always clear what needs to happen to access it – or even what 'it' is. Sometimes, it's not so much the unknown that pressures us, it's our fear of what might have to change to give way to the more that wants to emerge.

What *is* certain is that women are experiencing this as pressure: while there's a compelling force to move on, advance, change and ascend in life and leadership, there's also a strong conviction that it's safer, wiser, better somehow, to keep things the way they are – familiar and relatively comfortable in comparison to venturing onto the path of potential risk and disruption.

It's so uncomfortable to want something and not know what it is or how to attain it, especially after all the work it's taken to get to where we are in life and leadership. For many of us, our current position is working on so many levels, and, in any event, our bandwidth for disrupting the status quo has been used up. So we say to ourselves, *I don't have time to go messing up the routine.*

LEADERSHIP PRESSURE: IT'S PERSONAL

There are a couple of things I notice most about the pressure. One is how relentless it is, and the other is just how personally we take it. Also it's true that for many of us, pressure has become so familiar that we just expect it. We put up with it, tolerate it and let it have its way with us.

The pressure makes us feel unsafe, and then that becomes 'normal'. It undermines trust and so having no one to trust becomes 'normal'. It creates risk and so feeling at risk is normal. We say to ourselves, *This is just the way things are; this is just how work is.* It's easy to stop noticing how accustomed to it and how on guard we've become – all the time!

On a daily basis I witness the collateral damage done to us when we have to continually brace ourselves to face the pressure. Women are repeatedly mustering up the energy to resist buckling under it, and it's exhausting, draining and energetically expensive; it definitely takes its toll. We're burning out, we're breaking down, and we're punching below our weight. There's a quantifiable shift in the number of women I connect with who are suffering from physical conditions in response to the pressure, among them adrenal fatigue, migraines, insomnia, cancer, heart disease, fibromyalgia, all manner of autoimmune deficiencies and of course, depression.

FOUR RESPONSES TO PRESSURE

Some of us attempt to mitigate the effects of pressure, believing that if we can just try harder and do better, we may be able to conquer it and cause it to subside. When that doesn't work and our energy is used up, what do we do next? I've noticed that women in leadership respond to the pressure they face in four key ways: they shut up, they doubt their power, they quit, or they fight back.

1: SHUTTING UP

I've seen talented, insightful women with the experience and knowledge that could solve many of the problems faced by their organizations, gradually grow silent in response to the constant and unrelenting pressure they experience. Here's an example.

One cold January I was called by a woman who worked as a director for an NGO in Manchester. Her tone was as steely as the weather and I soon learned why. Her line manager, the CEO, had extended her probation period after complaining that she lacked gravitas as a senior leader; he felt she needed to step up and show up more. But at the same time, the CEO was continually usurping the woman's authority, making it difficult for her to do what he expected.

On one occasion she was tasked with leading a recruitment panel to fill an important project role within her team. Her boss had an idea of who was the most appropriate candidate for the post but he agreed that the recruitment process should be open and fair so that everyone interested would have an equal opportunity to secure it. My client interviewed all the applicants and, along with her panel, decided on the best candidate for the position. But when she presented their recommendation to the CEO, he was obviously perturbed that they'd disagreed with his own choice. My client was told to 'go away and rethink your decision'.

'I knew he wanted me to agree with him,' she explained anxiously. 'And in the end, I just did what he wanted. I didn't want to go against him. I didn't want to cause trouble.' The result? The wrong person was hired for the role, impacting both the team and the mission. Perhaps more important, however, was how broken, undermined and manipulated this woman leader felt. She told me she lost respect for herself and strongly suspected her team did so too. 'They watched me go against my own conviction,' she said. 'Any power to influence them has been fractured.'

The acquiescence broke her spirit and took with it her capacity to influence. Why hadn't she stood firmly for what she so strongly believed? After all, she had her team's backing and she hadn't made the recruitment decision alone. My client approached her boss to ask about funding her coaching with me, but he insisted that *he* would choose her coach. We spoke about her lack of choice in the matter: 'I'm the only black woman there,' she said. 'I don't want them to think I'm a stereotypical angry black woman.'

'But *are* you angry?' I asked her.

The volume of her voice lowered to almost a whisper: 'Yes I am. I'm angry now.'

'Sometimes the most influential thing you can do is to be honest in the moment,' I told her. 'The most appropriate thing we can do is honour our truth. But instead, we put it away, for the sake of acceptance, for the sake of not being seen as this or that.'

2: DOUBTING OUR POWER

Some time ago I met up with an old friend while she was staying in London en route to an international conference. Julie and I had been longing to have a face-to-face catch-up and celebrate her new role for months, but living in different countries had made that a bit of a challenge.

After decades of directorship in education, Julie had decided to apply for a regional director position in health and social care, and she'd got the job. I was so excited that I'd be able to find out how it was all progressing, but when we met I was struck by my friend's lack of enthusiasm. 'It's okay,' she said. 'It's been nearly eight months now and I've really settled in. The people are fine... the work's fine... everything's fine.'

I listened until I could do so no longer. 'All right, Julie, spill the beans,' I said. 'What aren't you saying? What's really happening?'

It turned out that my friend had been feeling a little despondent after her career move. She'd anticipated that the shift in industry and the new role would shake things up; she explained that she'd become a tad complacent, even a bit bored, in her previous role, and she'd hoped that the new position would put a little fire back into her life. 'But I find myself having the same conversations with heads of departments, attending the same meetings, writing the same reports, giving the same presentations,' she lamented. 'It's a different organization but exactly the same old stuff.'

As Julie told me about some of the characters she was working with, the politics, the game playing, the isms and the schisms, I noticed she barely talked about the organizational mission or her own personal ambition to make a mark and be the change. So I challenged her: 'But there's so much work to do – so much room for improvement. There's a great need for things to improve for the service users in your region. Isn't that why you're there? You've so much to bring to that role and mission, right?'

My heart sank as Julie began to tell me how important it was to be realistic about what was possible, that she was under no illusions and that it was the 'big boys' behind the scenes who were pulling the strings. Her job was, basically, dancing to their tune. 'I'm not the one with the power – they are!' she exclaimed.

Her words reverberated in my heart. Not only had I heard them from clients, friends and associates who lead at this level, but I too had also felt this way before. Julie isn't the only woman positioned to create real, meaningful, important change, yet feeling powerless to be the initiator, innovator and influencer of it.

3: QUITTING

Everybody knows that if you can't stand the heat, you get out of the kitchen, right? Well, many of us do get out, whether we actually hand in our resignation or just withdraw emotionally and stop engaging with or investing in our role in any meaningful or true depth – we'll talk later about quitting while staying in the job. Either way, organizations are losing out on the opportunity to benefit from the difference that a woman leader could potentially have made. But all too often, it's the only way women feel they can respond to the pressure: they give up by quitting or acquiescing.

I've seen women quit their leadership role and move on to do something else, walk away, or take sick leave so they won't have to work their notice period. Some women leave in a good and orderly fashion while others jump without a parachute and work out how to fly on the way down.

I remember having a conversation with a woman about quitting. She wasn't a client but we had a real and true, connected, naked conversation about life and leadership on the three-hour train ride from London to Plymouth. She told me that she'd walked away from her executive role in public service because of the pressure she'd been under.

'What are you doing now?' I asked her. She told me of her 'little children's party business': 'nothing too elaborate' was how she described it. She went on to explain that she'd always been good at throwing parties for her children and now that she was out of corporate, she'd found this to be a way to bring in some 'pin money' and keep her 'out of trouble'.

I felt sad that this brilliant, strong woman who, from the stories she shared and the way she shared them, still had much to offer the corporate world, had been so hurt by the pressure. She quite confidently told me, 'I'm just not cut out for the corporate space.' But then she added, 'I do miss it, though: I really did care about making a difference in public health.'

I know that feeling. In my position as a regional director, I'd actually quit some time *before* I handed in my resignation and left the job. This is the second way that women quit: the way we tend to think less about. We turn up every day and do just enough to not get fired and still get paid. In this type of quitting, we withdraw ourselves: we find some comfortable little corner in the organization and we just do the job. At this level, it's no longer about the people we're serving, and it's no longer about the greater good: it's about survival.

Women keep their heads down so as not to rock any boats, while their aspirations slowly fade out of their hearts. The embers are often *still there*, but they're barely detectable. I realized this when I woke up to the fact that I'd opted out of the pressure by finding myself that comfortable little corner, from where I spoke the words and did the things that showed I was being a good girl.

I realized I was killing off the part of me that was truly passionate about making a real difference to the people I was there to serve. On that day, it was as if I had new eyes: I looked through the glass walls of my office into the open-plan space, crammed with my colleagues and teams of other conscientious worker bees, and realized I had to get out of there or I'd die.

I've seen women leaders quit in both of these ways. The result is the same, though: we become unavailable to speak our truth and make more difference. Sometimes I wish I hadn't quit, although with hindsight I can see that the role wasn't my sweet spot. I was just passing through on my way to being prepared for the work I do today. Still, I can see how there was so much for me to learn about myself in that situation, under that pressure. Golden insights were mine for the taking, yet they were invisible to me at that time, when all I could see and feel was the pressure.

So many women in leadership feel that they *have* to stay in their role, and it can be such a conundrum to work out whether it's time to stay or go. What I know is that there's a big difference between running away and moving on elegantly, just as there's a difference between staying on elegantly and fighting our way into an early grave.

4: FIGHTING BACK

Quitting isn't our only problematic response to the pressure. Sometimes we perceive that the only fitting response is to stay in the position and push back; we're compelled to fight, saying, 'I won't be pressed, I won't be squeezed, I won't be this or that.' We walk around in 'fierce mode', insisting on, or even demanding, equality, fairness, access, respect and recognition. We want it because we know it should belong to us and we've made up our minds to fight back and take by force what's ours. Sometimes, way down the line when we take stock, we realize we're fighting in ways that don't serve us; we're fighting everything and everybody and it's exhausting!

Some years ago I was approached by an executive at a big accounting firm in Middle America who was interested in hiring me as her coach. She described with great passion her leadership aspirations to make partner within the next few years, but added that she was experiencing what she called 'extreme pushback' from some of her leaders. She suspected that they weren't too keen on having women in their C-suite and were being very cautious about how easy they'd make her progress within the firm. She assured me she was up for the fight and that she was going to find a way to win it.

I listened intently as she poured her heart out, but something was bothering me. 'Why do you want to advance to partner?' I asked. The question seemed to stop her in her tracks; I saw her go inwards, as if searching for the answer that had been put away somewhere a long time ago. Eventually, she said quietly: 'Money I guess, or maybe just the sheer accomplishment of it all.'

The point was right there for us both to see. She'd spoken with such force and conviction about her determination to 'fight' her way to partner, but actually she'd no real, heartfelt motivation for it, apart from proving a point and collecting another stripe. She wasn't short of money, had no children and had a very long and impressive list of accomplishments and professional accolades, yet there she was, caught up in a personally taxing fight with no real reason for the push.

Some of us are battle weary. Some of us have been fighting that ground warfare for a very long time. The evidence tells us we're more susceptible to burnout and job stress than our male counterparts, and I can't help but notice that when I get behind the masks of women leaders. We're becoming unwell and experiencing dis-ease; our marriages are suffering, our relationships are feeling the strain, and our personal lives are paying the price too.

The bottom line is backed by evidence: we're less happy now than when our fight for equality in the marketplace began. Sometimes I think we've lost our way, forgotten our point, stopped connecting to a higher purpose for why the fight's important – maybe we've never consciously connected with it.

Years ago, I decided to accept that half of the women who choose to work with me don't do so because they really believe in the power of coaching and talk therapy, or because they're happily seeking out alliances as part of their wellbeing and professional development strategy. Many of them resist reaching out for help for years, gritting their teeth and resolving in their hearts to carry the weight of it all in secret and silence. They eventually come to me because they've shifted from hunch to full-blown conviction that something's got to give or they're in for a very big crash.

I know this might make for grim reading and that we'd rather talk more superficially about how powerful women are now that we've made it to the top (which is true), but it's critical for us to face the other side of things too. We pay too high a price when we don't go behind those professional masks we wear and truly wake up to how the woman behind the title and the position is doing back there!

DESPITE THE PRESSURE, WE STILL CARE!

We've been talking about the pressure women leaders experience and the ways in which we respond to it. Yet despite it all, we still care – we still want to make our difference! The embers of the vision that led us to leadership in the first place, coupled with our care for the people we're here to serve, still burn within our hearts.

A few years ago, a social media post written by a brilliant woman caught my attention. Pauline Tomlin is a department head and part of the senior leadership team in her school, and I'm aware that she's conscientious in her work and passionate about education as a means for changing the world. Here's what she said:

> As an educator, I'm often conflicted. I hate the homework and I don't see the point of it when I know the pupils need rest. But the terms of my contract deem I do as requested in the execution of my duties. So they're given three pieces of 40 minutes per night if they're in KS3 and so on. I can't keep up with the bloody marking anyway and, through this and the half-termly testing, I end up wrecked through lack of sleep. Testing what?! As a teacher I get great results, but for what? For whose benefit? I stop myself often and ask, what the hell am I doing?! Unfortunately, the system is so ingrained that everyone buys into the [concept of] 'first past the post' and A-grade outcomes. It's okay in its place, but it's not for everyone. I guess I'm in crisis. I can't keep doing this.
>
> I love the pupils I teach. I adore getting them to see their potential and reaching for it. They talk to me. I see the spiritual being in them and speak to that. I hug them (shhh... not allowed!) I teach them meditation. I talk to them about life and sex and money and friendships and loving themselves. I want to create environments children literally 'run' into because every moment is one of creativity and connection and joy. The question is, how? It's time!

It touched my heart when I read this. I felt a connection with the woman from whom these words flowed. I perceived her frustration, desperation even; this is a true leader, a change-maker who's ignited from the inside – despite the pressure and systemic holdbacks – to make a difference through her work and leadership.

This leader cares enough to impact her world in the way her heart and her eyes tell her is necessary. She's not alone. Every day I meet, talk to and work with women who lead at high levels in the marketplace, across sectors, and they echo the same sentiment: 'I'm conflicted. The system is failing, and failure is so ingrained. I still care, but I don't know what to do. I don't know how to change the system!'

While this is a strong sound coming from many of the women leaders I meet, there's another sound I hear from others. I recall a phone conversation with a client some years back in which we discussed a recently published report that highlighted worsening crime rates and lowering educational attainments in her region. This woman, a CEO of a national charity connected to the justice system, spoke with fierceness about how awful things had become and how sad the report made her feel.

'What needs to happen?' I asked her. 'How come you care so much? And how is it that you lead in this field and yet things are getting worse?' She paused before answering and then said, 'I don't know. I think we need to find a completely new approach. And while I really *do* care, I just don't know if I have the energy to take on anything else. I just don't know where I'd find the time!'

We went on to have a deep conversation around this, and I heard her gasp as if in fresh realization as she asked and confessed simultaneously, 'I've become complacent, haven't I?' We spoke about how caring wasn't enough – it wasn't the push she needed to get involved. She'd had a lot on her plate at home after her marriage had broken down, leaving her a single mum with three teenage children. However, her job was, in her words, 'cushy': she could be flexible with her hours and do the work itself without any real challenge; everything was pretty predictable year in year out.

There was no doubt that she cared, but getting involved in the fight to fix the broken system she'd identified as the root cause of the problems in her community seemed like too big an ask and too big a risk to the clockwork routine that made life work for her and her family.

I left that call with mixed emotions. Of course I got where she was coming from – I'm a mum too and I believe that family must come first, period! But I couldn't help feeling a little sad too. I know that so many of us who are positioned in senior roles and have the authority to challenge the broken system that perpetuates our giant societal problems and challenges feel the same. Despite the pressure, we all still really care – but not enough to disrupt our lives and be the initiators of change that would *really* make a difference.

It's a picture of dashed hopes, and yet, as I reflect on the experiences of these women and the many others like them, I marvel. I'm heartened that through it all, despite the pressure, we still want to make a more meaningful impact in our organizations, industries and, ultimately, our world. Something deep inside still compels us to want to make that difference, even if we don't know how, and even if we don't feel that we can afford what we perceive it'll take.

The question is then: how do women like us handle our desire to make a difference in spite of the pressure we face? How do we express our care without it costing us too dearly? Is there a way forwards? Can we still make a difference?

CHAPTER 4

THE KING NEEDS
A QUEEN

Let's begin this chapter with a recap of what we've covered so far. We've been talking about the marketplace and the powerful system that governs it, which is made up of people who lead, people who follow, people who buy and sell, and people who create and trade. It's a complex human system – one that I've proposed is like a king: a powerful sovereign entity.

This marketplace system, or the king, has a personality, a spirit, idiosyncrasies, beliefs, a culture, rules, codes of conduct and opinions. Some of these are written or spoken, while others are known only in tacit, mysterious ways. We've been exploring how this system, this king, perpetuates, creates, sustains, maintains and impacts inequality, which in turn impacts and hurts human lives in a myriad of ways.

We've looked at inequality as a psychological structure, a way of thinking, in the collective mind of the king. And we've seen that while anyone can have thoughts that conflict with the king's biases, and while anyone has the right to think of themselves as equal to anyone else and we all have the right and the responsibility to pursue success according to what we believe is possible for ourselves, the reality is that it's hard to be immune to and resist the king's biases.

For some people, it's hard to progress in a system that works in ways both visible and invisible to hold them back, or to keep them down or out. A system that sees them as less than, or inferior in some way – even when they know that's neither right nor true. So we examined some of the ways that inequality shows up and how it affects our wellness.

Under the rule of this king, people don't like their jobs, they don't like themselves, they don't like their lives, and they don't like each other. Trust is low, resentment is high and separation, segregation, stress, isolation, competition, scepticism, exclusion and game playing are just a few of the ways we respond to the inequality that exists among us.

We talked too about the imperative for the king, the marketplace system, to experience a change of heart: we need a king that understands and celebrates people – a king that genuinely refutes the lies of inequality, which see some as inferior and others as superior. We need the king to wake up spiritually and receive the revelation about the power that will be unlocked and unleashed when *everyone* has the opportunity to walk according to their true potential and their unique greatness.

We need a king that understands the laws of abundance and genuinely sees the benefits of wholeness and wellness at all levels for all people when they feel valued and loved and significant.

We know the king understands this intellectually, but that isn't enough for true change to take place: the king needs a genuine motivation to do the hard work and the heart work required to create the shift from inequality to equal opportunity and equity for all. The king needs to receive a revelation of this truth from his heart.

As I said earlier, we can't *make* the king change his mind. We've seen the various methods that have been tried, some of which *appear* to be successful, namely women's ascent to senior leadership positions. However, while it's true that we're slowly winning the battle for equal access, attitudes towards women in the workplace suggest there's still a long way to go for the king to truly and wholeheartedly appreciate and facilitate the difference that women make. Likewise with black and brown people and other minorities.

We can't hold a gun to the king's head and shout our insistence that he sees people differently. At best, that creates politically correct behaviour and ticks for tick-box exercises. It doesn't work to beat this king into submission. He needs a far more elegant and sophisticated influence: one that doesn't overlook his power; one that doesn't disregard or disrespect his position or make him feel defensive and dishonoured. A powerful influence that's respected and even sought out by the king himself. *This king needs a queen.*

QUEEN ESTHER

A great example of a true 'marketplace queen' in action can be found in the Bible's Old Testament. The Book of Esther tells of a young Jewish girl who lived in Susa, capital of the Persian

Empire, with her cousin and mentor Mordecai 100 years after the 6th century BC Babylonian Exile (when the Israelites were forced to leave their homeland). As the story unfolds, we see that Esther hides her Jewish identity and moves into the royal palace to become one of King Ahasuerus's concubines. Later she's chosen from among them to become the queen of Persia.

Haman, one of the king's highest officials, is promoted, and he issues a decree that everyone should bow before him in reverence. When Mordecai refuses to bow before Haman, the official is furious, and when he finds out that Mordecai is Jewish, he persuades the king to issue a decree to annihilate the Jews. The king agrees, the date is arranged and 11 months later the Jews are set to be murdered by the Persian army.

Esther becomes the Jewish people's only hope. She and Mordecai make a plan for her to reveal her true identity to the king and influence him to reverse the decree. Although Esther is queen, approaching the king without his invitation is an act punishable by death. It's a huge, scary risk, but Mordecai, knowing how Esther must have felt about taking it, sends word to the girl, letting her know that she too will be affected by the king's decree to kill the Jews. Mordecai urges Esther to realize that she's been promoted to queen for the sake of her people, saying: 'And who knows but that you have come to your royal position for such a time as this?' Esther 4:14.

The story goes on to reveal how Esther curried favour with the king and was therefore able to persuade him to issue new decrees that allowed the Jews to escape with their lives. She'd prepared herself and courageously went before the volatile king, saying, 'if I perish, I perish'. Her heart was set on the mission to save her people.

Mordecai's words to Queen Esther, 'for such a time as this', resonate deeply with me. It's a beautiful turn of phrase that's so relevant today. Mordecai was talking about a time and season of great risk to his people. His point was that Queen Esther's positioning in the king's palace wasn't an accident, or random, but divinely timed to make an incredible difference to the Jews. If Esther hadn't been in position and if she hadn't understood the call on her leadership to intercede and influence and bring the plight of the Jews to the king's attention, they were due to be annihilated throughout the empire.

THE CALL TO WOMEN WHO LEAD

We're being called to ascend to our thrones and take up our position as queen in our respective domains – you and I and our fellow sisters who lead around the world represent hope for the king. *We* are his chance to be powerful and productive and to command a healthy competitive edge without the need to compromise the health and wellbeing of his citizens. Think about it: the queen is the one closest to the king. She's privy to his mind, she sees behind the scenes, and her access to the king is unparalleled. My truest conviction is that it's us, you and I, the women being called to be queens in our industry, organization and field, who are being chosen and commissioned by God himself to influence the system within which we lead.

We're already in the palace; we're already connected and close to the king. We're at the board table; we're part of the conversations that shape culture and policy; we're involved in the way marketplace decisions are made. We're already powerfully positioned to influence the king and now we're being divinely called to prepare. We must grow in our capacity to revive the king's heart, his humanity, and his compassion. We have this window of opportunity to evolve to a whole new dimension of influential capability – like the biblical Queen Esther who so powerfully influenced the unreasonable King Ahasuerus.

The king needs to remember how to love again. The king needs to reconnect to his humanity. At the root of the word 'human' is compassion, and there's no compassion or love or truth in inequality. The truth is we're equals as human beings; we're all equally valuable. This isn't an intellectual shift – it's a spiritual awakening, a soul revival. And I strongly believe that womanity was made for the job! Now we must take our place as the effective influencers of a radical shift in the way the marketplace king relates to and impacts his people.

PREPARING TO TAKE OUR THRONE

The Bible clearly and strongly states that Esther went through an entire year of in-depth preparation before she was allowed to go before the king. She was given fine oils, lotions, potions and cosmetics to make her skin soft, sweet-smelling and beautiful; she ate the finest foods to nurture her inner health and wellbeing; and she was given staff: seven other women who supported her and took care of her every need. She also had a mentor who taught her the ways of the king and palace protocol. Esther *prepared* to be queen of Persia and partner to the king.

We're being called to do the work, to go through our own preparation process, to ready ourselves to stand up and present our hopes, dreams, aspirations and visions for the important, meaningful change we want to see in our organizations, industries and fields. We must prepare to make our requests, declarations and decrees with elegant and undeniable power and influence, and time is of the essence.

It's true that we have a seat at the C-suite table and a pipeline is being created to ensure this continues to be the case; but I'm proposing we accept this call to higher influence and take things further. It'll require us to rethink who we are, why we're at the table, and what we bring to the marketplace. This is a new paradigm for being an Influential Woman in leadership.

It's a kinder mission, one that doesn't require us to burn out or sabotage ourselves to survive; it's one that calls us to enter into a league of our own. This mission celebrates our womanity and authentic feminine expression as an asset, rather than something to be masked, hidden and ashamed of. In fact, it requires an 'unmasking' of our womanity. It's a new, woman-centric approach to leadership, an inner game – one that'll result in a win for women who know there's more for them to be, do, say, create, express and experience in their world. It's a win for the marketplace, its stakeholders and the greater good, too!

Accepting this mission also means accepting the call to evolve and develop, to grow, mature and take our place as the influencers we're divinely intended and urgently needed to be. Dealing with the pressure and all the plates we're spinning and all that we've experienced in getting to this point has been part of our preparation process. We've already been getting ready; however, we can't stay where we are: we need to go beyond our own personal fight for equality and see that it's our positioning in marketplace leadership that makes us ideal champions for the people in our realm.

We must grow and evolve in our capacity to see ourselves as influencers of the king. This is the work of our lives. We need to ascend to a whole new level of commitment to influencing the king because this is more than just about us. This is a global issue; it's about impacting and curtailing the way that the marketplace feeds inequality.

BECOMING A QUEEN INFLUENCER

Ascending to your throne as a Queen Influencer is a process. As I see it, as leaders, we go through three phases of evolution. The first phase is Child Influencer; in fact, we don't ever stop being a Child Influencer. This phase is when we learn about influence – we see how influence happens, we're taught how it happens and we absorb information like sponges, learning how things get done, how what goes goes, how things become established. We learn who's in charge and how leadership happens around us; and we're fed information about how influence happens.

The second phase is Young Woman Influencer. While Child Influencer says, 'Show me, give me the tools – influence me!' Young Woman Influencer asks, 'What can happen through me? What can I do? What can I make happen?' Young Woman Influencer is very ambitious. She wants to showcase her influence; she wants to try it out, to see what she can make happen. And she wants it to be attributed to her: she wants to be seen as an influencer and make a name for herself. In this phase we're fighting for status, we're fighting to be seen as the one who says how things go. We want to showcase our leadership and our influential prowess. We want to prove our ability to make things happen.

Then that young woman grows up. She matures as an influencer and as a woman and ascends to the third phase of influence – Queen Influencer. Queen Influencer sees her sphere of influence as her domain and considers it her life's work to care deeply about the wellbeing of all who reside therein. Her role is to partner the king: working closely alongside him, influencing his decisions, and helping him to stay on track with his sovereign assignment.

Queen Influencer contemplates deeply the needs within her domain; she takes seriously the role she plays and her responsibility to ensure the king meets those needs. She's no longer driven to impress anyone. She's interested in impact, in the wellbeing of the king and her people. She wants people to thrive, and she wants her community, her domain, to be good, to be well. She cares about the people in it, and she realizes that only together can they all be well. She thinks of herself ultimately as the one with the greatest influence with the king and sees it as her responsibility to support the manifestation of the potential of the whole.

The Queen influencer is wise and prudent. If the king is the head, then she's the neck, determining which way the king is looking, what he's seeing and desiring for the future of their domain. Where the king is preoccupied with displaying his power with quantity – bigger, faster, higher, more, more, more – Queen Influencer brings quality to the plans of the king and sees her leadership as the catalyst for not just productivity, profit and competitive advantage, but wellness and quality wholeness throughout their domain.

The Queen Influencer has a mother's heart and she owns her power and her responsibility as an influencer. Influence isn't merely something she does: it's *who* she is. She has influence and favour with the king; what she says carries weight and she directs this power dutifully towards desired outcomes. She rules closely alongside the king, working in partnership with him for the good of the kingdom, their domain. In the queen's heart are these questions: 'What do my people need?' 'What's possible for us?' and 'How do we make our domain great again?'

BEING QUEEN IS OUR DESTINY

It's no accident that you and I are women who lead right now. I'm convinced that we've come to this place, at this level of seniority, within this sphere of influence, at a time when people's lives and liberty, safety and wellbeing are at such great risk. We need to influence the king to act for the good of all. We need to be modern-day Esthers, prepared to be courageous and go before the king to contend for change on behalf of the people and challenge his unrighteous decrees.

I'm convinced that our history has been setting us up to take our queenly positions. In her book *7 Traits of Highly Successful Women on Boards*, Dr Yvonne Thompson, a woman and mentor I admire deeply, talks about her migrant journey to the UK. She and her family were originally from Guyana in South America and they went through so much in that season of transition before

Dr Yvonne could take her place as one of the first women leaders to sit on a UK board and make way for so many others.

In her book she says that our experience as women in leadership is similar to that of the migrant journey. Consider this: there was a time when there were no women in marketplace leadership – it was a men-only domain – but we're here now. The journey hasn't been smooth and it's been slow and sometimes painful. Think about what womanity has survived across the centuries, and right up to the present day: we've been treated as chattel, used, oppressed, abused, attacked, silenced, stripped, burned at the stake, overlooked, scandalized and underestimated.

I think about the women I work with and the real stories behind their professional success – stories of survival, fight, grit, shame and guilt. Some of us got here by the skin of our teeth: I think of the massive battle that has raged within me, driven by the knowing of my greatness yet so bound and held back by the lies of what it means to be a black woman in a white man's land.

Womanity has survived! We've travelled, we've travailed, we've pressed and we've climbed. We've strived, we've tolerated, and we've waded through the shit and the storms. Collectively and individually, we've made it to today. As far as I'm concerned this is down to the hand of God. Providence has moved on our behalf. Womanity has been supernaturally guided, protected, covered, shielded and brought to this place where we are leaders in our domains, where we are in such close proximity to the king.

I don't know what it's taken for you to get where you are today in marketplace leadership, but what I can tell you is that it's miraculous that you're here. Women's presence in the marketplace, and this call to be queen, is a divine and timely imperative. And it's not only for the benefit of the king and the people – ascending to queen, leading and living as her, is our birthright, our inheritance; it's what it means to fulfil our destiny.

This is the work that everything has been leading to – all that we've suffered, gone through, fought for and endured. It's the work that it's impossible for you to leave undone if you're to have a fully lived life. It's the work of your destiny and it's of personal, global and generational significance.

IT STARTS WITH US

If you're still reading, I'd say that's a pretty big clue that we go together – that this message is for you. You're a woman being called to evolve and grow and ascend to a new dimension of influence with the king. You're being called to facilitate the king's healing and transform his output and outcomes.

If that's to be, there's a process involved, and you're being invited to take it. To become her – the leader, the influencer of our potential and in fact our destiny – there's work involved. As I've engaged with this work, I've found that what I hate most about the system, what I most want to change about the king, *exists in me too*. I've learned that if I want to ignite my authority and power to influence the king's transformation, I have to start with my own transformation!

If inequality, racism, genderism, ageism, injustice, indifference and unfairness are in the king when I find myself responding to them 'out there', it's usually pointing to something in here, in me. I'm not exempt – if the king is resistant to new points of view, then that resistance resides in me too; if the king is ashamed then shame is in me; if the king is oblivious and indifferent, then those things operate, consciously or unconsciously, in some form in me too. I've learned this and have chosen to accept it.

If I see it in the king, I choose to find it, face it and address it first within myself. I've found that as I seek it out in my own heart and choose to handle its manifestation in my own life and leadership, I grow, I evolve, and I ascend in my capacity to support the same in the women I work with. I've found that handling it in my own heart and mind leads me to be qualified, prepared and equipped to address it in my realm of leadership.

This isn't always easy work to opt into. It can be hard to accept the ways inequality and unfairness show up in me. Often, the very things I don't like in the king operate on stealth mode within me, or feel normal, justifiable and right. It's when I see it out there, in the king, that I can see clearly how wrong it is. It's easy to blame and point it out in him.

I don't know if this is invariably the case; I don't know if it's as true for you as I've found it to be for me. Maybe there are things happening within the heart of the king that don't operate in my heart or yours. But when I'm working closely and behind the mask with my clients, and when I'm doing my own work to evolve and develop myself as an influencer and leader and change-maker, I haven't yet found an undesirable quality in the king that isn't mirroring a potential or actual expression operating in me – within my own soul, thoughts, behaviour or responses.

I've learned that if women in leadership are going to evolve as the kind of influencer that can truly touch the king, disrupt his malfunction and transform his reign, we must do the work ourselves. If the king needs healing then so do we; whatever the king needs, *we* need. Whatever's in the king is also in us.

THE SEVEN HABITS

This work requires us to face things about ourselves – both those things worthy of celebration and those things that are painful. I'm fully persuaded that it's the only way to become the kind of influencer that people are crying out for and that the king so badly needs. When we do this work we by default heal in ways we didn't even know we needed to; we by default learn new ways to be. We unblock new waves of understanding, compassion, passion, empathy, courage and resolve – and it's from *this* place that we can stand before the king on behalf of the people: unafraid and unapologetic.

When we do this work, we're able to look outside of ourselves and understand afresh what the system needs in order to change, what the king needs in order to be restored and realigned to his sovereign duty to care for the people. It's from this place we become allies, exemplars and champions of the healing process; we become undeniable and irresistible models of the new ways to win.

I'm not suggesting we should spend our time searching for our faults and weaknesses and beating ourselves up over them. What I *am* saying is that we should do the work by intentionally developing *good habits* – those that support our healing and unmask our blind spots and the aspects of our character and leadership that hinder our ascension and evolution as sovereign influencers. Good habits that'll ignite our capacity to be seen, heard and taken seriously by the king.

So in Part Two of the book, I share the seven habits I've been intentional about cultivating on my journey – those I've found to be the most fundamental in my ongoing transformation as a change-maker, a queen and an evolving influencer in my domain.

Part II

The Seven Habits of a Queen Influencer

RADICAL AUTHENTICITY

W*ho are you?* This is a question we seldom ask the people we work with in any more than a superficial way, and it's definitely not a question most people ask or answer for themselves. And yet, of the seven habits I'll share with you in this part of the book, radical authenticity is perhaps the most important one to master. It serves us to become intentional and habitual about knowing who we really are and to master the art of showing up as her in our leadership and life.

Radical and authenticity are two words I love – *radical* refers to the fundamental nature of something or someone and *authenticity* means to be genuine, original and true to one's own personality, spirit or character.

In Part 1 we spoke about the fact that although as individuals we're largely good people – we care about fairness and we favour the creation of a level playing field – when we get together within our respective workplaces within the global marketplace what we co-create *still* manages to be unequal, unjust, imbalanced and unfair.

In this chapter, I'd like you to consider that at the root of this dysfunction in the marketplace is *inauthenticity*. Although as individuals we're conscientious about change and transformation, when we take up our positions as leaders within the marketplace system, it doesn't translate. We struggle to show up as our *real* selves, as different and distinct, and instead we're obsessed and preoccupied with blending and fitting in. We're reluctant, even terrified, of standing out, and we work hard at acting how we're 'supposed' to instead of how we're being 'called' to in the name of transforming results.

As I reflect on my life, I can see that radical authenticity is the deepest lesson I've been called to learn and the one that's been the most challenging to establish as a habit.

My Life Behind the Mask

I sat looking in the mirror, a million thoughts pumping around inside me with every beat of my racing heart as I tried to make sense of the unfamiliar reflection staring back. Behind me, to my right, stood Mr Marmion, the white-haired surgeon whose hands smelled so strongly of hospital soap; he'd known and cared for me since my birth. To my left stood my mum. The three of us gazed, transfixed, at the 'me' in the mirror.

It was a special day because I'd just been given the most important gift of my life. It wasn't a new dress or a toy, as you might suppose, considering I was just four years old. No, my gift was an artificial eye: a smooth plastic shell shaped like an eye and painted the same colour as my good eye.

After being born with a harelip, a prominently asymmetrical face and blind in my left, poorly formed eye, I spent a lot of time in hospital having corrective surgery (I'm sure this was the reason I became a midwife). As long as I'd known myself, I'd thought of myself as 'disfigured'; my appearance had always been an issue, and I was very aware of how different I looked, how abnormal I was.

I'll never forget that day, staring into the mirror after the surgery to fit my new eye. I'll never forget that feeling of searching to recognize myself, looking at the 'me' in the mirror and waiting for that sense of familiarity to kick in. As I write this I can feel that odd, visceral sensation that came with not knowing me. 'There you go,' said Mr Marmion, beaming. 'Now you look beautiful!' My young mind took in his words. *Well, I'm not sure about beautiful, but I guess I do feel a bit more normal. Am I normal now?*

That was the beginning of my life behind the mask. I know it wasn't intentional, but what that artificial eye (and later, a pair of dark glasses) taught me was that when something about you is different – when you aren't the same as everyone else – you hide, you take steps to blend and fit in, you do what you have to do to be like everyone else. I learned about the undesirable nature of being different; I learned that the real me was different and that if I wanted to be beautiful and fit in I needed the help of my mask. And that's how I lived my life… until 2009, a year of seismic events.

THE CALL TO RADICAL AUTHENTICITY

In January 2009, Barack Obama became president of the USA, sending the world into a frenzy – a black man was moving into the White House! In my circles this was *massive* news. Before taking office Obama had fought for the leadership of his party against a woman, so at one point, the very real prospect that the world's most powerful nation could be led by a woman or a black man played out before us. Wow! Everyone was saying there was something very, very special about that time and season.

That month it was also announced that the UK was officially in recession following the financial crisis of 2008. Then, later in the year, Michael Jackson died. That entire year, Hillary Clinton, Obama, Michael Jackson and the economic crisis seemed to dominate the news and *every* conversation! And, in the midst of it all, I noticed I was becoming increasingly agitated. At first, I didn't know why, but I soon realized that something was jarring, deep inside me.

Every time I had a conversation about those super-achievers, people seemed to see them as 'other': as if they possessed a gene that made them a different standard of human. Don't get me wrong, I admired Obama and those other geniuses immensely, and was hugely inspired by their lives, but I was struggling with the inference that our world is made up of amazing folk at the top and then 'everyone else'. What bothered me, I think, was my growing awareness that I'd probably be in the 'everyone else' category!

Then came the Dalai Lama with his famous proclamation: 'The world will be saved by the Western Woman.' I remember the night it dawned on me that *I'm a Western Woman and so are my clients!* Shortly afterwards, in true Law of Attraction style, I bumped into three former clients within very quick succession, and on each occasion, the exchange went something like this:

Me: 'Hi! How are you?'

Client: 'Great, thank you! Long time... must be a year since we last spoke.'

'Yes. How are things going – what happened with your plans for this and that?'

'Um,' followed by too long a pause. 'I'm still in the same place. I do still think about some of the things we spoke about, though.'

After the first encounter I wondered what had happened to this client. She'd left our sessions feeling like a new woman, as if she could take on the world, so where did all those plans and that fire *go*? After the second encounter I started to feel deflated. By the third, I began to wonder what the heck was wrong with me! How come my work wasn't producing sustainable, meaningful, powerful change in the leadership and lives of my clients?

I became very aware of the knowing in my belly that I too was called and capable of great exploits. But something inside me was objecting, vehemently, to the evidence that I might be a member of the 'whine and blame all my failures on the economic downturn crew'! It was a challenging, confusing, inexplicable internal battle between the part of me that was saying *No! This isn't it for you – there's more! You're greater than you know right now* and the part that secretly struggled so very much with believing all that.

If I'm so great, I thought, why am I playing so small, and why isn't more changing? Why aren't I having the impact I long to have? Why is it so hard to advance and grow from where I am? I know I've done well, but I don't feel done. I'm so dissatisfied! And right then, at the point of my highest frustration and struggle, my aunt died.

REFUSING TO LET LIFE GET IN THE WAY

Aunty Tiny was a really special lady: she had class, style and was very intelligent. Although she'd trained as a nurse and was a keen seamstress, her real flair was for teaching. Aunty Tiny had the capacity to turn any conversation into one of her teaching sessions. Education was her calling and we children could all tell a story or two about the mandatory maths and English lessons at her house during school holidays.

Aunty Tiny had been living with leukaemia and renal failure for some time, and when I visited her a few days before she passed away, I hoped she didn't notice my audible gasp when I saw her gaunt frame. We spoke candidly about God and faith. We talked about life and her illness, and about death. We sang songs of praise and thanksgiving. We laughed, we cried, we hugged and held hands.

I told her how amazing I thought she was, and how I'd often thought that she was living way beneath her potential. I told her that I'd often sense that she could change the world somehow, become famous, win awards for something, make history. Aunty Tiny listened to me and smiled knowingly. Although she didn't say so explicitly I sensed her agreement; she knew it was true. But she told me, 'Dion, life just has a way of getting in the way.'

I remember the look on her face as she said this to me, and as I do so there's a voice inside me, urging you and me to promise to refuse to 'Let life get in the way' of who we could be! Then she was gone. I cried at her bedside and ached that she was no longer with us. We loved and would miss her so much. And secretly, I ached that the world out there would never again have the chance to be touched by this amazing woman's light.

Let's make a promise right now, you and I: 'I promise I'm going to make the difference I was born to make. I promise to touch my world with my gifts and my talents, to share my unique insights, and to bring unique solutions to real problems. I refuse to hide, suppress, blend in, or get caught up in mediocrity, traditions and the humdrum of work life. My world will be different because I lived and worked.' Go on: I dare you to say it out loud!

SHOWING UP FOR REAL

In the days following Aunty Tiny's passing, things were hectic, with people coming from near and far to express their condolences and to celebrate her life. And I still needed to work…

One evening, I drove 120 miles to be with my family and host a gathering. Jay, an old friend I hadn't seen for decades, was there. We'd known each other in our teens and had parted ways when I moved to London. It was good to see her. She had a 10-year-old son, and he sat with us as we giggled and chatted, catching up on the news of the previous 30 years! But her son was so irritating; he kept fidgeting, making funny noises and generally getting in the way of our longed-for conversation. 'Keep still! Be quiet! Can't you see I'm talking?' Jay eventually snapped at him.

What happened next felt like a punch at a sore spot in my heart and boy did it hurt. 'She's ugly, Mum!' the boy exclaimed, pointing at my face. I felt hot, shame hovered over me, and palpitations arose. But then, something strange happened. I noticed that I hadn't flinched at his words – it was as if I were a spectator at the scene. Inside, my heart was wounded, but on the outside, I was as cool as a cucumber and you wouldn't have been able to tell what I was really going through. *How do I do that?* I wondered.

The next day, as I stood in the foyer of my church, some children ran up and tapped me on my shoulder from behind. When I turned around, they pointed at my face, laughed and ran away. The pain was mounting. Throughout that week, similar incidents delivered punches that would trigger memories of growing up with a facial disfiguration. But the worst one occurred on the day of my aunt's funeral.

That morning, I lost my dark glasses – they were part of my mask so it freaked me out! I was certain I couldn't attend my aunt's funeral without them, but my family insisted I go, and my sister kindly lent me her sunglasses. I realized that recent events had left me feeling sore. Each time someone looked at me, I'd recoil and want to cry, 'Please don't look at me!' I was so aware of these thoughts and feelings and, as if for the first time, I knew something was up. I was hurting.

The morning after Aunty Tiny's funeral, my three-year-old niece found my artificial eye on the dresser by my bed as I slept; she'd not seen me without it before and it was too much for her young mind to fathom. When I woke up she was back in her room. I went to speak to her but she wouldn't look at me, and she didn't want me to touch her either. Silent tears streamed down her face as she cowered in the corner of her room.

That was the final straw. All the pain that had been brewing that week exploded out of me; I thought I'd die from it. I did the only thing I could: I ran to my room, fell to my knees, put my hands up in the air and said out loud: 'God, what on earth is happening to me? It's hurting, God. Help me!' In that moment I entered into a conversation with God, and the familiar voice in my heart began to speak: *Dion, what's all this hiding about? Why are you covering yourself up? When are you going to show up for real? When are you going to let people see the real you?*

As I wrestled with the questions I was being asked, I realized the truth: deep inside, unconsciously, I believed that my face, the real me, who I really am, wasn't a good thing to expose or inflict on people. It felt cruel to make people look at and see the real me. Up until that point I'd had no idea I was thinking of myself in this way. Facing my own thoughts was a big, painful deal.

I don't know how long I spent on my knees that day, but by the time I stood up I'd made a decision: I was going to find a way to drop my mask and master the art of showing up in my life, my work and the world. I decided to let people see the *real me*. And I was petrified.

REMOVING MY MASK

Today, I can clearly see how pivotal this experience was for both my leadership and my life. At the time, it was a deeply personal, private and painful process that life had thrust on me and insisted I yield to and endure. In the days, weeks, months and years that followed, I embarked, step by step, on the road to my own becoming.

I couldn't see that this experience was connected to the deep frustration that had intensified in me in 2009, in the wake of

Obama and Clinton and Jackson. I didn't imagine that life was teaching me the foundational principles that would catapult my capacity to teach and support my clients in the sustainable ways I longed to. I'd no idea that it'd open my eyes to a key that can potentially change our world for the better forever. But that's exactly what was happening.

Across all my social media platforms, I took down my profile pictures – those images of me with an artificial eye and dark glasses were a lie. But now that I was stripped of my mask I didn't know what I looked like. I couldn't bring myself to get in front of a camera and have more photos taken, so my profiles stayed faceless. I was still posting, but a logo represented me while I started to make sense of what I was going through.

I sent a request to join an online women's business forum called I'M WOMAN. When the owner, Cheryl Bass, asked me to describe who I was and what I'd bring to the group, I said something casual, like, 'I'm passionate about developing women.' But Cheryl kept pressing, 'Yes I hear you, Dion, but *why?*' After she'd asked that a third time, I thought, this woman's really asking to know me, for real.

I sat with that for a moment and I remember how it felt: I could feel my awareness rising and my soul catching up with what had been happening to me over the previous few years. Then I ran to the cupboard, dug out my video recorder (no iPhone back then!) and for 15 minutes I spoke to camera about what I'd been going through: my conversation with God, the decision to drop my mask, all that I was learning about the power of showing up for real.

After I recorded that video I was literally shaking like a leaf – I knew in my belly that if I shared it, I wouldn't be able to take it back. It felt risky, stupid, unpolished; I wasn't ready, and as I uploaded the video from my camera to YouTube, conflict raged within me. *Post it... No, don't!* But I also started to experience tiny sparks of excitement at the thought of other women hearing what I had to say. I'd not heard anyone talking and sharing in this candid, naked-truth way.

That video went viral. I couldn't quite believe the response: women from around the world commented on it, shared it and sent me messages. Something about my story resonated deeply with theirs. These weren't women with facial flaws like mine – they were beautiful women, smart, savvy women; they were black, white and brown women from all walks of life who were moved by what I'd shared – enough to want to tell me what *they* were going through.

I began to teach them, and they began to teach me. We began to learn the real story. I began to see women all around me who were hiding too. Things began to change in my interactions with my clients. The way I questioned them was different; what I'd look for and see was forever deeper. My perception was sharpened – my interpretation of leadership, my own and theirs, had profoundly shifted. And the more I shared my story, the more women connected with me and told me their truth – about just how pervasive masking had become in their life too: these smart, brilliant women with great accomplishments, powerful titles and roles and professional stripes.

I've learned so much about the metaphor of masking: what it is, how I wore masks in so many ways – hiding myself and not showing up on so many levels of my life. Playing small, shrinking back, stepping aside, dumbing down, punching way below my weight, both professionally and personally as a woman, leader and change-maker. Most of all, I learned that you can be a woman at the top of your career game and still be quite unaware of the masks you wear, why you wear them and what you think about the woman you're trying to hide.

As I did my own work, I discovered that in the process of growing up black and disfigured, I'd thought of myself as ugly, unlovable and a huge disappointment. As I faced these unconscious thoughts and self-perception, they explained so much about the struggle I've experienced with feeling like an imposter in senior leadership.

A life of physical masking had taught me how inappropriate the real me is, and how inappropriate and even detrimental it is to let her be seen out in the open. I came to find out that the metaphorical masks my brilliant women clients were wearing in their leadership roles were teaching them the same thing.

Learning from Being 'Not That'

Over and over in our professional lives, we interpret events through the masking experience. We believe that our truest selves and ideas are simply not welcome and should be put away where no one can see them. This is what happened to me in the aftermath of the Faith in the City event I described in Chapter 2 – when those disapproving men in suits stood at the back of the audience. I felt vulnerable, defenceless and very 'swat-able'. Expulsion felt imminent, as if I were now a target.

I'd been well and truly put in my place. I found myself a little corner within the establishment and made a conscious decision not to rock the boat ever again. For three long years, any sense that I was positioned to bring forth my ideas – those that contradicted the zeitgeist – diminished, and I'd little sense that I was there to influence.

I learned the reality of the giant power structure, the king, of which I was a part. I learned how things were 'done around here'. I learned who was in charge and that it sure wasn't me. I felt as if the king had let me into the role and that he'd let me take home some money every month and allow me to sit at the board table, *provided* I stayed with his flow.

Although I was the director of the programme I led, that programme fitted into a giant power structure, within which I was a nobody – I didn't matter. I was in the room when decisions were made, policies set, culture shaped and plans devised, but my ideas and insights about what needed to happen for our families became insignificant as I donned my armour, rolled up my sleeves and got on with busying myself, doing what I needed to do to look as if I belonged and was sufficiently worthy to be paid and not dismissed.

I was under stress and pressure and felt so insecure about being me. I'd lost my connection with the truth about my innate value and all that made me an asset and qualified me to bring value to the table. I was a faceless, personality-less, powerless worker bee who did what was expected of me. Or at least that's what it felt like.

I went to the meetings. I spoke the lingo. I wrote the reports. I did what I needed to do. I aligned myself with the agenda of the powerful and spoke their words – sometimes almost parrot fashion. I nodded, smiled, clapped when it was appropriate. I played the game. And they nodded, smiled and patted me on the back.

What was happening here? I had a high title but a low sense of self as an influencer; a big position but, in my own thinking, little power to actually contribute to and shape the kind of difference and change we all said we wanted to see, and which had led me to apply for the role in the first place. I was underestimating my power as a response to the pressure to conform. I felt intimidated by the king, as if I was powerless. It wasn't true, but in believing it, it became true – true and *inauthentic.*

I say that inauthenticity goes a long way towards explaining how it is that the king goes unchallenged, and how he's unchanging and unequal in his outcomes. Inauthenticity causes us to shut up when the opportunity comes to speak out; it causes us to say yes to things that in our hearts we should say no to, and no to things we should say yes to.

Showing Up Authentically and Influentially

Decades after that day in Mr Marmion's office, I remembered the feeling of staring at my four-year-old face in the mirror when I sought the help of a business coach to grow my business and build my brand to make it more visible to new prospects and clients.

The coach explained that everything I use for my marketing should look like 'me': 'People want to know who you are, Dion,' she explained. 'People buy from those they know, like and trust.' I learned that everything I chose should represent me: from colours and fonts to platforms and pictures. But what the heck did that mean? The coach asked questions designed to help her pull my visual brand together: What colours do you like? What words describe you? What do you stand for?

As the questions came thick and fast I felt a growing sense of anxiety. Hot, quiet tears began to form in the corner of my eyes and despite my efforts to hold them back they rolled down my cheeks, proclaiming my shame and discomfort: here I was again, sitting in the realization that I don't know who I want to be. I don't know how to show up as me in business, and I don't know what it means to be me in the public eye.

Today, from my privileged position working alongside many brilliant women in leadership, I know I'm not alone in feeling this way. I've learned that you can be a woman at the top – a celebrated CEO, a dedicated director, an accomplished head – and still not know what makes you *you*; you can still be worried and clumsy about how you're coming across; and you can still be emotionally invested in trying to manage what others think about you and being what you think is expected.

We can become so caught up with trying to 'act' our way through – trying to be like the professionals over there or to behave in the way they expect over here. It's exhausting, and if we're going to advance as influencers we must quit trying to be what they want or what they say is expected of us and commit to finding out who we really are. And then be ourselves instead.

It's time to take seriously the call to show up for real – the call to recalibrate, to get back to centre with our true selves, to realign with who we really are. Our development as influencers of the king calls us and demands that we show up to leadership with radical authenticity. It's painful to not know, or lack confidence in, who we are. When there's ambiguity, anxiety or identity crisis, it makes showing up, authentically and influentially, a real challenge.

I've come a long way since that day in Mr Marmion's office. I've been on an incredible journey of self-discovery, and I'm still on it. I've reinforced that commitment I made back in 2009 to show up for real. I've learned how to get to know myself, and in turn I'm learning to let you and the outside world see and know me too.

DEFINE YOUR AUTHENTIC LEADER IDENTITY

If we're going to evolve as Queen Influencers – if we're going to ascend to a whole new dimension in our capability to impact the king – we must unlock our power to influence by aligning with who we really are. And yet there can be so much confusion in our minds and in our thinking about what it means to truly show up as 'me'.

We must commit to finding, facing and embracing our real selves. We must be as intentional about getting acquainted or reacquainted with ourselves, and do so with as much fervour, as we are when we're falling in love or developing a relationship. When we meet someone new, someone we're interested in spending time with, we ask them chit-chatty questions: What's your favourite colour? What's your favourite food? When were you the happiest you've ever been? When were you the most afraid?

We ask a million and one questions like this. Why? Because we want to know that person, we want to understand who they are so we can learn who they will be to us, and how we can get the best out of them and the relationship. We ask those questions to obtain clues about our compatibility with that person – their responses help us work out what we need to give in the relationship to make it work.

A successful relationship should work like a ship – it's supposed to help us move on, advance, go forwards – and nowhere is this more important than in the relationship we have with *ourselves*. This is why we need to invest time in understanding our true selves and defining our authentic leader identity. So, as I do with my clients, I invite you to ask yourself the following questions…

WHO WERE YOU?

I love to remind my clients that they came here as someone: the 20 years I spent welcoming babies into the world qualifies me to say this with conviction and certainty. Let me tell you the story of the three babies who reminded me of this.

One night on the labour ward the doors swung open and the ambulance crew wheeled a woman towards us. As soon as we midwives laid eyes on her we knew she was on the verge of giving birth. I waved the ambulance crew towards a vacant room and then greeted the woman and asked her what was happening. She could hardly get her words out: 'I'm in pain,' she said. 'I think I'm in labour.'

'I think you might be right,' I told her with a smile. 'Anything else I should know?' I asked routinely as I helped her onto the delivery bed. 'I'm only 30 weeks pregnant,' came the reply.

'Oh! That makes this a whole other situation,' I said, pulling the emergency buzzer and beginning to make my assessments. 'I'm having triplets!' the woman announced, her breathless words heavy with fear. Thirty weeks was way too early to be birthing and three babies added significant risks and complication – this was an emergency and it wasn't long before the room was filled with an entire team of professionals ready to receive these babies.

I parted the woman's legs and there it was, the head of triplet number one, advancing fast. I positioned myself to deliver him and within a few minutes he was in my hands. He seemed to be in pretty good condition considering the early gestation. I tried to interpret the look on this little one's face: he seemed so full of wonder and fascinated by his new surroundings. It was as if he was saying, 'Wow! Where am I? What's that? Who are these people? This is so cool!

I smiled and prepared to deliver triplet number two, who came without complication. This baby seemed totally unimpressed. He was in a bad mood – as if he was demanding to know who the heck's idea this was. Didn't we know he'd been having a nap? It felt as if this baby was insisting we put him back in his comfortable place right away and leave him alone!

Then it was time for triplet number three. She was altogether different to her brothers: cool as a cucumber, she wouldn't have looked out of place if she'd arrived sporting a pair of Ray-Bans! She seemed decidedly unbothered, unflappable, unimpressed and unafraid. Her personality was strong, and I *felt* her. As I cut the cord, this little madam grabbed my arm. Our eyes met and for a moment it was just the two of us in the room. She was captivating. We connected and right there in that moment, I *knew* her.

I think about that triplet and her brothers often, and what they helped me to see – that we come here as someone; we're born with nuances and personalities; we have an identity in the womb. Think about that for a minute – who were you when you came here? I often encourage my clients to dig out newborn and early life photos of themselves and just stare at them, thinking about the identity of the child and who she was before life happened. I've seen such powerful things revealed through this exercise. Many women experience a falling into place, where they learn or re-see things that are and were true about themselves from the womb.

OUR GENETIC INHERITANCE

This really struck true for me when I met my Uncle Bobby – a brother that my father didn't know he had. My dad and his own father had parted ways after an argument when my dad was a teenager. After my dad left his homeland, Jamaica, to join his mother in the UK he never saw his father again.

Fast-forward to a few years ago, when a family friend visited my father's house for a dinner party and brought along a friend from the USA who was staying with her. My dad had never met this friend, but he opened up his table to receive her as his guest. They started talking and as usual when Jamaicans get together they began exploring their roots. Which district did you grow up in? Where did you go to school? Who were your parents? When it was my dad's turn to share his information, the woman's jaw dropped: 'I know your brother Bruce!' she exclaimed. 'He's my neighbour!' She immediately pulled out her phone and called a number in the USA and my dad then spoke to the brother he hadn't seen since he was 19 years old!

That incident opened up a whole new family for me. Apart from Bruce, my grandfather had gone on to have three more sons, all of whom had families of their own; I've inherited a host of uncles, aunts and cousins. It's been tremendous, but the best thing was meeting Uncle Bobby, because we just clicked! He shared stories about my grandfather, whom I never met. I learned about his entrepreneurial pursuits, his style and poise. With every story, I saw myself, and I saw my father and my sister. We're like him and he's in us!

Getting to know about my grandfather has opened my eyes afresh to the mystery of generational inheritance. We don't come here empty – we're laden with the opulent histories of our ancestors. So often we're heavily focused on our generational curses. I meet women who recount the less desirable traits in their ancestors: 'All of the men in my family are alcoholics', or 'All of the women die of breast cancer'. But what about the greatness that has flowed through your family's bloodline to you? What about the resilience, the inherent skills, the gifts and talents, and the positive traits and characteristics?

It's so powerful and important to reclaim and remember these as you commit to radical authenticity – they're a part of being you. It's time to consider what reviving and bringing these traits into your leadership and life would look like.

When I did the 'Who Were You?' exercise again recently, I realized for the first time that just as I didn't develop conventionally in the womb, so it is now – I'm still unconventional. I don't do leadership development like anyone else. I'm unconventional, and knowing and embracing this about myself helps me to deliver my own radical authenticity. There's no one like me. And there's no one like you, either.

WHAT'S YOUR NAME?

Another great place to look for clues about who you came here to be is your name. What does your name mean? How did you come by it – what was the thinking behind your being given that name? This one enquiry has brought such light to so many of my clients as they seek to realign who they're being with who they actually are.

Like the client for whom a recurring theme behind her biggest challenges was that she automatically saw everything through a negative lens. Then she discovered that her name means 'beautiful eyes'. It was so profoundly meaningful to discover this and it offered up new dimensions of context: often in our coaching session I'd intuitively find myself saying to her: 'You need new eyes.'

Or the client for whom the word 'defeated' kept coming up when we explored how she was showing up at work; she discovered that her name means victory. Or the client who, after realizing that her challenge as an influencer was rooted in a deep and hidden belief that 'nobody cares about me', discovered that although her name didn't bear a particularly positive meaning, it was a thoughtfully considered one given to her by her father. That spoke in a very beautiful and metaphorical way about just how loved, wanted and cherished she'd been on her arrival.

What is there for you to discover about yourself in your name? Those wonderful things about you when you got here are still you, still true. On our path to radical authenticity we're being invited to re-embrace the truth of who we came here as.

WHO ARE YOU NOW?

The second dimension of enquiry about your authentic self lies in who you are today – now that you've walked a while, now that you've gone through what you've gone through, worked where you've worked, seen what you've seen, learned what you've learned. How has your journey so far shaped you and made you who you are? What do you value? What are your needs? Who are you now?

When I took a client through this exercise recently she discovered what so many others have done when committing to this level of enquiry: that she'd stopped being interested in self-discovery. It had been way too long since she'd spent quality time with herself, getting to know herself. In fact, when I suggested she do that, her first impulse was to reject the idea, calling it 'frivolous navel gazing'. But when she warmed to the idea what she discovered was priceless – the way she'd been thinking about herself had been, in her own words, 'outdated'.

It was as if a light went on and all at once she could see that although she still thought of herself as the woman she'd been at 30, actually, here she was in her early 50s. She'd gone through dramatic shifts in terms of her life and leadership experience and *everything was different* – her children had grown up, her marriage had ended, she'd been promoted extensively, and her social life had been transformed. Everything that is, except her thinking about herself. This was a huge revelation and it had a knock-on impact on everything.

I invite you to put aside quality time to ask yourself, 'Who am I now?'

WHO ARE YOU BECOMING?

One of my favourite client organizations is the UK's Ministry of Defence, and over the years I've had the great privilege of working with some of the extraordinary women who lead in the Royal Navy. One of the many things they've taught me is that if you shift the direction of a ship by even one degree, over time that ship will end up in a completely different, but predictable, destination.

What they're really saying is that trajectory is a powerful predictor of destination – not only with ships but also with leaders, with people, even with organizations. In other words, if you study your journey so far, if you look back and see the themes, connect the dots, recognize the patterns, you can use this information to look ahead. You can use it to determine what the future looks like if you stay on this path.

I encourage my clients to think about their habits, their patterns, what they read and listen to, the people they surround themselves with. I ask them, 'What's your morning routine? Where does it look like you're headed? Who are you becoming?'

UNLOCK YOUR POWER TO INFLUENCE

Radical authenticity requires us to pay attention to *her*: the woman, the leader, the change-maker yet to be revealed. She's already in you and she wants to emerge, and who you are now is the doorway through which she'll make her appearance. She's the *you* in waiting, just like the beautiful butterfly in a caterpillar.

There's some of her that we won't or can't yet know. I like to think she's hidden in God, snug in the womb of time awaiting her arrival, but she can and is reaching out to us. She lures us forwards, calls us home to the woman and influencer we live to become, the purpose we're destined to fulfil. If only we weren't so damn busy, if only our world weren't so loud, we'd hear her, see the signs that lead to her.

In your commitment to radical authenticity I implore you to listen, to see the signs, join the dots, visualize her and seek her. She's calling out to you, cheering you on. She'll help you to find yourself and be more you now in the service of becoming more you in time.

I often ask my clients, and now I'm asking you, to spend time with her as a way of making this connection with the woman you're becoming. Be as curious about her as you are about anyone, perhaps more so. Finding *you* is finding your power to influence, and the beginning of showing up and being you in leadership. You cannot be who you don't know, and being the real, influential you is so much more beneficial to the king and the people you serve than acting like the person you think you're expected to be.

Repowering Our Womanity

It's imperative that we understand what it means to be a woman, and how we can use our power to influence the world in which we work, lead and serve. It's time for us to understand our womanity and bring it to our leadership roles with courage and conviction. So in this chapter, I'm inviting you to consider womanity. What do you think it is? Why do you think it's important, or not, in leadership?

Understanding My Womanity

My curiosity about the question 'What is a woman?' was aroused at the age of 10. I recall standing in front of the bathroom mirror, looking deeply into my own eyes and feeling very embarrassed. I can see myself now, and feel the feeling as if it were yesterday.

My mum had asked a portrait photographer to visit the house to take some shots of me with my little sister, Denise. I was feeling apprehensive – I hated having my photo taken, being disfigured and all, and especially since to my mind, Denise was so pretty. So I guess it must have been anxiety that made me do what I did. As I got dressed for the occasion I felt an unusual desire to wear a bra! I don't know where this idea came from and it's baffling that I decided to follow it through. Our cousin Carol was staying with us at the time, and I rummaged through her clothes to find her bra and then put it on beneath my long purple flowery dress.

Before the photographer arrived my mum called me for the obligatory inspection: she fixed my hair, rubbed cream on my face, smoothed down my eyebrows and made sure my earrings were securely in place. When she began straightening my dress my heart started racing. I didn't have a relationship with God at that time, but I'm pretty sure I prayed: '*Please* don't let her find out I'm wearing Carol's bra.' God couldn't have heard me though because my mum clocked the empty bulge of the bra as it struggled to lie as flat and un-contoured as my chest.

'What's this?' she asked, as if irritated that the dress, despite her manipulations, wasn't behaving itself. Then, as if in slow motion, she reached under my dress and located 'exhibit bra'. She was so livid, she struggled to form a complete sentence: 'What... Why... How?' She ordered me to go upstairs and 'take that off', using the voice she reserved for the times we'd been really, really naughty.

So there I was, in front of the bathroom mirror feeling embarrassed, confused and frustrated and wondering what the heck I'd been thinking. I looked at my reflection and gave myself a very stern (though loving) talking to: 'Look, Dion, there's no way you're going to be a real woman. Men aren't going to fancy you or fall in love with you and be romantic. You're not wife material. But don't worry, you'll be okay – you've got other things going for you. Just get used to the idea!' It was the best advice I could give myself. I took off Carol's bra and re-joined my family to have the portraits taken.

Something else happened in that same bathroom around this time. Again, my embarrassment-o-meter is off the scale right now but here goes. I'd overheard a conversation in which a woman who'd recently given birth described the pain of labour as 'like wanting to go to the toilet really bad!' Somehow, that had captured my imagination and so there I was again in the bathroom, this time sitting on the loo bursting to wee. I let myself start to go and then squeezed my pelvic floor muscles tightly, so the wee stopped mid-flow. I remember basking in the sensation of my bladder's objection and the way I held the flow for as long as I could until the 'pain' was at its peak. I remember drinking in the sensation, eager to experience what it felt like to give birth. *So, this is what labour feels like. I think I could do it! I think I could have a baby!* The thought was strangely exhilarating.

As I think back on these two events, I see a young girl secretly grappling to understand what it means and what it feels like to be a woman. Today, I see how womanity has been consistently important to me throughout my career and in my own journey of self-discovery, but back then I had no idea why.

It was after 2009 – my turning point year when I made the decision on my knees that I was going to find a way to show up for real – that I realized I'd have to figure out what it means, for real, to be a woman. After all, that's who I am: being a woman is an integral piece of my authentic identity. Understanding my own womanity had become a real priority.

THE GENESIS OF WOMANITY

For me, it makes sense to think of womanity from a spiritual perspective first. I subscribe to the premise that we're spirit beings who have a soul and live in a body in order to have a human experience. If that's true, then surely we need to develop a spiritual intelligence about what it means to be a woman.

When I want to understand something important I turn to the Bible, the foundational resource of my faith. This ancient book is packed with clues about God's idea of and for womanity, and woman is a strong feature in the scriptures. They describe how at Creation, God brought forth out of a dark void a very special land in whose eastern corner He planted the Garden of Eden. He populated this garden with all kinds of life in the air, sea and land. He planted every kind of tree, herb and flower, and when it was complete and looking fantastic He crafted and created His masterpiece: mankind.

God created Adam (in Hebrew Adam means human) and put him in the garden He'd created for him. He said (and of course I'm paraphrasing), 'Here you go, Adam: I'm giving you this domain. Be Lord of it. Whatever you say goes here. It's teeming with everything you need. I want you to take care of this land and allow the land to take care of you.' It sounds to me like God made Adam the king of the garden: 'If you look after it, it will look after you and you can live in perfect harmony with it.'

And so man, Adam, received and became lord of his dwelling place and it was good. The Bible describes how man named the animals and tended the land. Until something changed – that which God had thought good started to display the need for innovation, improvement, enhancement. Something was missing, lacking, needed. Something was not okay.

GOD'S MODEL OF DUAL LEADERSHIP

In my wild imagination, I loved to see God stroking His chin, shaking His head with furrowed brows, wracking His Sovereign brain about what He was perceiving as He watched mankind lead in his domain and realized that this picture wasn't complete. I wondered what it was that led God to conclude that His creation was falling short of His expectations for good. I'd often ask God in prayer, 'Reveal it to me, Father… show me what you saw that led you to bring forth *womanity*.'

Then I saw it, written in the text that had been right under my nose the whole time. God said, 'It's not good for man to be alone.' My excitement grew as I grabbed my Bible dictionary and searched for the original translations to better understand this: what did it mean that man was alone? I then discovered that in the same passage of scripture, the Bible describes how man was not alone but would walk and talk with God in the cool of the day. In fact, the garden, man's dwelling place, was equivalent to God's presence; and yet God worried that man might find himself alone – outside of the presence. I was intrigued.

The clue lay in the language. Hebrew, the language of the original biblical text, is rich and each word is associated with a picture. In Hebrew the word alone means separation, and the picture it paints is one of something falling away from its source, the thing that gives it life – like a branch that's become disconnected from the tree or the chief of a city disconnecting from the source of his assignment and authority to lead. Could that be suggesting that Adam was at risk of struggling to stay connected to God as he dwelt in God's presence, led and was lord and king of his domain? Was he struggling to remain connected to Love, to Truth, to Light, to the source of Life?

So the story unfolds that God went back to the drawing board. He didn't start from scratch in the creation of humanity – He enhanced it. He addressed the glitch. He got over the presenting problem with innovation – the *innovation* of man. He extracted the best of man's heart and fashioned Man 2.0, producing Woman! From Adam God brought forth a 'helper': equally man but different, equipped to ensure that man would not lead in his domain disconnected from source, from God, from Love, from Life, from Good, from Light.

Wow! It was hugely exciting for me to glean this understanding from the scriptures. Womanity born out of divine intention to keep humanity connected to source – to Love. Woman was innovated and that means she's not a different creature: she's fully man, fully human, but distinctly fashioned to help humanity stay connected to its true source and rooted in Truth, Love and Light.

For years I've heard and read the disgruntled, irritated, even angry words of those who have suffered at the hands of what I call 'the fake patriarchy' of male domination: those who interpret the term 'helper' as inferior, second-rate, beneath. But you know what? I've never heard anyone explain what exactly women are here to 'help' with. Indeed, the confusion around this point is phenomenal, and over the centuries women have been treated as chattel and slaves as a result of a gross misrepresentation of the term helper. Now here it was being revealed to me in the scriptures and everything made so much sense.

Woman was brought forth to influence humanity to stay connected to God. It was an act of God's Love for humanity and a divine expression of Love: a conduit for His Love here on the Earth. And man was to become one with woman – the part of himself that knows how to stay connected to the source, the part of himself that accesses the way for a full, successful life and the preservation of all life in the garden. I like to think of their union as the divine plan for leadership success because when God joined them together His instructions were clear: 'Be fruitful, multiply, take care of your domain. *Together.*'

Womanity was made to *help humanity* to fulfil its assignment to look after the garden, to be fruitful, multiply, subdue, replenish and have dominion on behalf of God and in God's way. Or let me rephrase it: on behalf of Love and in Love's way. Womanity was the conduit through which Love would touch the Earth.

I think of Adam and Eve as a type of senior leadership, and their appointment shows that God's intention for leadership requires man and woman to come together to produce what's required for the wellbeing of the domain.

WOMANITY IN THE BOARDROOM

A few years ago, I was invited to speak to a cohort of women at a business school, all of whom were in senior roles: leading in their own right, training to improve their chances and secure their seats at the board table as chairs, executives and non-executives. Each desired to advance her position and be an effective decision-maker.

During my session, which was called 'Authentic Board Leadership', we discussed the word 'authentic'. First, I shared my definition of it: 'When your thoughts, words and deeds are lovingly aligned with the Truth of who you are.' In other words, showing up for real and leading in a way that's genuinely aligned with and true to ourselves. The women agreed with my definition.

Then I steered the conversation towards unravelling what it means to be 'authentically woman'. What does it mean to be authentic as a woman at board level? As you can imagine, the discussion that transpired was a heated one. There were four loud sentiments coming from the women in the room. The first was: *Yes, I'm a woman, but I'm not going to let that stop me!* This implied that being a woman is a drawback or an impediment. The second was: *There's absolutely no difference between me and my male colleagues!* The third was that being female, feminine or womanly isn't something to be celebrated or shouted about in the corporate space: *not if you want to be seen as equal.*

These women told me that their aim was to be acknowledged in the same way as men. They despised the idea of being seen as different or distinct because they're women. One acknowledged that although there's a 'big difference' between male and female, she wouldn't show up at work in her true feminine way because 'These people would eat me for breakfast!' Finally, the fourth sentiment was the admission of huge uncertainty around the benefits of being a woman in leadership.

These sentiments aren't as uncommon as you might think. For some time now, I've been running and developing a very special retreat, exclusively for women in senior leadership, called the Leader's Lounge. It's a place where women in corporate positions of influence and leadership come to take off those professional masks we all wear at times and take a real look at what they're facing, professionally and personally.

In the Lounge, women think, review, redefine, refresh and evolve as leaders and change-makers, and it's 'an extraordinary experience' (their words, not mine). Their candour and courage are beautiful to see and an honour to be a part of, and it always amazes me how particular themes emerge, unifying the women in the room.

Recently I ran a Leader's Lounge in-house session for a national organization in a heavily male-dominated industry. Five senior women attended, and during the discussion one of them kept repeating the phrase 'overtly feminine'. It came up as we talked about ways to respond to things at work. The woman said that for her, it wasn't enough to have the title of leader – she wanted to be *seen* and *acknowledged* as being good at her job, and being 'overtly feminine' was *definitely* not perceived as something that would work in her favour.

Every woman in the group nodded and knew exactly what she meant. I saw and heard loudly how these women were making daily decisions to dumb down, hide, mask and conceal the truth that they are indeed *women*. I listened as each woman confessed and recounted story after story of how she'd put away her *inner woman* in a bid to be seen, heard and taken seriously as a capable, credible member of the organizational leadership. I'm using the word 'confess' deliberately here to express the sense of embarrassment, even shame, that I sensed behind the women's words.

And to be honest, it's no wonder. The world is confused about the power and value and importance of womanity. We're bombarded with loud, conflicting messages about who we are and who we're supposed to be, and it's easy to conclude that being a woman is all about having babies, having sex and having (or not having) a good dress sense. It can seem as if we're judged on our body parts – on our breast and bum size – how well we apply make-up, how high our heels are, how high-pitched our voices are and how emotional or not we are.

I'd seen and heard this many times before but this time it seemed louder. Right then, I found myself wondering – and I'm inviting you to wonder along with me – what kind of impact it could be having on women's wellbeing, our performance and our potential to go up against the giants of inequality and injustice to forge a new and more influential relationship with the king.

If at some level of consciousness we're plagued by the sense that one of the core parts of our identity – being a woman – is thought of as inappropriate, inadequate, a threat, undesirable, unwise and contrary to success in the eyes of those we work with, how could that be affecting us?

As I write this it's bringing up the conviction I feel *every* time I encounter a woman who's semi-ignorant of the undermining implications of this way of thinking on our womanity at work. Time and again I'm struck by how uncelebrated and misunderstood womanity is among us. But here's the thing: if *we're* confused about our womanity and its value in the marketplace, it follows that the *world* is confused about womanity and our value in the marketplace. That's why I say it's imperative that we do the work to understand ourselves.

WHAT'S DIFFERENT ABOUT WOMEN?

Womanity is a divine endowment, a capacity to love others. Where there's womanity, there's love, nurture and care for others. Womanity brings forth new life. She beautifies and makes things qualitatively better. When I think of womanity as the conduit of love, I think of love as the power or fuel for care, nurture, healing and wellbeing.

Ultimately, it's up to us to teach the world the way of love. I say that where there's no love, womanity is malfunctioning: no love in the home; no love in the community; no love in organizations; no love in industry; no love in nations; no love in outcomes; no love in policies; no love in the culture. Women have an innate capacity to love: it's there to help us care profoundly and know, intuitively and deeply, things that are important for us to survive, thrive and succeed. It manifests in the way women think and know what to do, even when we don't always know how to explain it.

It's not that men can't do these things. It's not as if men don't have the capacity to know, care and love like this, but I've come to know it as inherently womanly. I like to say that women are the natural, divinely appointed stewards of it. Women are divinely created, chosen and called for this office. It's deeply in us. It's there to help us care profoundly for someone other than ourselves and to know intuitively what to do for the good in a way that's almost inexplicable.

Womanity has a divine assignment to bring forth new life, make things qualitatively better, nourish and nurture and beautify. Why are we the divinely assigned keepers of this work? Why am I so convinced that we're the selected stewards of this mandate and therefore equipped for it? As I explained earlier, I feel my career in midwifery has gifted me a privileged behind-the-mask pass to womanity. I've had so much opportunity to see her. I've experienced the mystery that I call womanity and its power.

As my professional competence grew and I became more skilled, little by little, my sense of womanity was shaped with every woman I met. I noticed, first very unconsciously and then increasingly consciously, I was becoming aware of the distinctive beauty and infinite capacity a woman has to take on the hardship of labour so selflessly for the sake of the new life within her. I'd watch each woman as she engaged through perhaps the most womanly deed of all: pregnancy and childbirth. That's when I'd see it: that unifying essence, that powerful capacity I now call womanity.

I've tried for a long time to find words to describe it, and still I cannot do it justice. It's not a logical or linear explanation and definition. I've found what I'm seeing and learning difficult to explain; I've found my understanding of it challenging to articulate. And yet, I feel compelled to try in an attempt to open your eyes and awaken womanity in you.

I saw 'it' in women from every walk of life – rich and poor, black and white, young and older, natives and migrants. I'd notice 'it' as women yielded and gave of themselves to accommodate the needs of the life within them. I saw 'it' in a woman's capacity to handle the pain of the process that would bring forth fruit, for the love of that fruit.

It was then that I began to recognize her, womanity, as expansive, strong and mighty, the embodiment of love. I'd notice her capacity to close her eyes, go deep within and know things – what her baby needed, what she needed, what was best in the present moment and in the long run, and how she could dig deep into what seemed like a bottomless reservoir to be the best for her child, regardless of the cost to herself.

I witnessed her capacity to stretch out of shape and expand to give way to the new expression of love (which is what a baby really is) that was to come forth. I witnessed her capacity to bring forth the new, miraculously, to make things qualitatively better, and to know things before they were logically knowable.

In the context of the labour ward, it's perhaps obvious that men readily see and appreciate womanity's power too. I enjoyed looking for recognition of it on the faces of the men who accompanied their women in the labour room. Sheer awe, that's what it looked like to me as men watched their partners go through the most womanly act of their lives. I've heard so many men comment on the mystery and marvel that is woman. They know that it's different, distinct, divine; they know its powerful pricelessness and peculiarity. I've heard so many men comment on how men just couldn't, wouldn't and don't have the same kind of capacity they see in womanity.

WOMANITY: THE MISSING PIECE

Despite all this, women still struggle to garner such acknowledgement, recognition and appreciation of our distinctiveness within marketplace settings and leadership. We've underestimated and undermined womanity in favour of the more masculine driven-ness, numbers, goals and targets, profits, gains and wins; things the way they've always been. I see so much behind-the-mask shame, uncertainty, resentment, ignorance, indifference and even intolerance towards womanity and her mandate in the world and in the world of work, particularly in public service.

But what if womanity is actually the key to influencing the marketplace king? What if the feminine is exactly what needs to infiltrate our systems to make them more equal, fair and just? What if womanity is the missing piece in the mission to create a transformed world?

The clues about the power of womanity to heal and know and make things better are everywhere – not just in the labour room and the nursery. Think about the power the feminine has to soothe even the most distressed man, and the way she can see invisible, catastrophic consequences and steer her family away from them. Some call it women's intuition, while others say it's neurological wiring. Whatever it is, I can't help but wonder what would happen if we could bottle 'her' and bring her to the boardroom, to power platforms and decision-making tables in public service. How could inequality stand a chance? How could injustice prevail? How could unfairness persist? And yet...

I've come to appreciate the intriguing paradox that despite this awesome strength, womanity is also so very fragile. It can be bullied, manipulated, undermined and disempowered. Whenever I think about this, my friend Jenny comes to mind. Her story is very close to my heart and I'm so grateful to her for allowing me to share it with you.

Jenny's Story

On our first day at the Bristol Royal Infirmary, Jenny and I got chatting and we just clicked: we were both starting as nursing auxiliaries, both living with our parents and both planning to stay in the role for a year before pursuing a nursing career at the same hospital in London. After we'd completed our training and relocated, our lives went in different directions and we lost touch. Then, some years later on the labour ward I spotted Jenny's name on the patient board; she was having a baby.

I skipped with excitement to her labour room, but as I entered I realized that something was up. The room felt hot and clammy and worry hung in the atmosphere. Jenny looked exhausted, and in her eyes I saw sheer hopelessness and fear. The midwife explained that the situation was becoming urgent, so I took my friend by the shoulder and said, 'Jenny, you've got to get yourself together. This baby needs to come out now!' I'll never forget the pain in her reply: 'I can't, Dion. I don't know how. My body's not working.'

'Yes, you can,' I told her. 'You were born for this. I'm going to help you.' Together we huffed and pushed and willed, and baby Sebastian was born after what seemed like an eternity. Jenny and I cried and hugged, knowing that something important had just

taken place in our relationship. But it wasn't until later that we got a chance to really talk.

Jenny had been delighted to be pregnant with her first child, but when the doctors grew concerned that a chromosomal disorder might be present, she was referred to researchers who were running a clinical trial. They strongly recommended a series of tests, but Jenny didn't want them: her instincts told her they were unnecessary. She described how the medical team wouldn't listen to her, though: they'd known what was best for her.

Reluctantly, Jenny had taken the tests. It turned out that the baby didn't have the suspected chromosomal disorder, but he was born with a developmental defect in his left hand and arm. Jenny's instincts had been right. She was devastated and felt drained of her power to protect the life she was carrying. She was certain that one of the tests had caused the deformity, but that couldn't be categorically proven. Nevertheless, Jenny's womanity had been usurped and undermined, and there, in that labour room, it'd been apparent for all to see.

Jenny told me that the guilt and power-drain of the pregnancy had 'switched her completely off' in her mind. She'd been so afraid of giving birth to a baby with a defect – for which she blamed herself – she simply hadn't been able to go forwards. So intense were the guilt and shame of not being able to do right by her baby, that the processes to bring Sebastian forth just shut down and Jenny had felt powerless to do anything about it.

This story still brings me to tears, and I could give many other examples of the devastating impact of disempowered womanity.

I'm convinced that centuries of usurping, undermining and overlooking womanity, especially today in the marketplace, is a big part of why so many of us wear multiple masks just to survive in our relationship with the king. But here's the thing: if women are to be the initiators, innovators and influencers of the kind of change we need to see in the marketplace, we simply must commit to a whole new level of understanding and leading in our womanity.

We must do this if we're to heal and convince the world – particularly the king – of our worth. I'm calling for a global re-understanding of the power and function of womanity. I want to see women embrace and understand who we are and what we have to offer. Only then can we unmask and unleash our greatness onto the world.

PREVENTING THE FALL OF WOMANITY

One morning during my jog in the park, I noticed a large fallen tree and felt compelled to go to it. This once magnificent tree lay prone and parched in the hot sun, and I thought about how beautiful it must have been before its demise. I imagined lush green leaves shooting out from its now bare branches. I imagined how it would have rivalled the beauty of any other tree that stood nearby.

And I wondered what had happened to cause it to fall. Maybe it had been a storm; maybe it'd been felled by those who'd decided it was in their way, an impediment; or, for some reason or other, it'd served its purpose and had had its day. I don't know why the tree had fallen but there I was, witnessing that indeed it *had*.

As I mused on this, my thoughts turned to womanity. I thought about the sound I've been hearing in recent years: the one I interpret as the call for the fall of womanity. This tree, in my thinking, became a picture of the agenda and intention that I perceive in my heart when I watch and listen to misguided, self-interested and often politically motivated groups of people calling for the fall of womanity. They're saying: 'She's outdated, and we don't need her. We don't want her. Gender is a fabrication. We don't need male or female – we're just humans, and there's no need for gender distinction.' This sound is gathering momentum.

As I pondered all this, I sat on the old fallen tree and felt sad. As I looked down I saw lots of little canisters and other drug paraphernalia littered about. It all made sense: I could see with the eyes of my imagination that this fallen tree was where people gathered to get high, to enjoy a different, drug-induced reality. And then it hit me: this fallen tree was a warning, a caution of things to come if we persist in calling for womanity's head and heart to be served up on a silver platter.

We must *not* kill her off – instead we must *fight* for her. We must *not* allow her to be felled – she is divine; she is God's gift to humanity. Nothing good can come from a fallen womanity. Let's fight for her. Let's heal her. Let's defy the call for her demise. Let's do the work necessary to discover how to bring her brilliance to public service. I'm committed until my dying day as I cry: 'Womanity, be understood, be unmasked, be unleashed. You're the key to a transformation in your industry.'

HABIT #3

RECONNECTING WITH YOUR GOD

A few years post-2009, as I began to unmask my faith in social media land, I had a powerful conversation with a Facebook 'friend' who told me how moved she'd been when I'd shared what God and being in church means to me. 'I'm not religious and I definitely don't go to church,' she explained, 'but I do go to the mountains – the mountains are my church.' She lived in Chamonix in France and Mont Blanc was virtually on her doorstep.

'Ah, what happens when you're there?' I asked her, excited at the comparison between church and the monumental beauty of that snow-capped mountain. She paused and then with eyes glistening she announced, 'I meet with my God.' To this day, the memory of that conversation fills my heart with joy.

However, I haven't always actively sought a connection with God. In fact, as a child I thought that God had a gang from which I was excluded because I didn't fit in. My grandmother, who was our carer when my mum went out to work, was a very spiritual woman, but she and I didn't always see eye to eye and sometimes we fought. She thought I was way too mouthy, too feisty. She'd sing a song that became a family favourite, sung with fun and laughter at every gathering. Here's the chorus:

> *How are you going to cross Jordan, Dion?*
> *How are you going to cross Jordan, Dion?*
> *Your hymnbook's lost and your prayer book's lost.*
> *So how are you going to cross Jordan, Dion?*

The Jordan was the river that stood between God's people in the wilderness and His promise of a land flowing with milk and honey. A hymnbook and a prayer book were needed to cross the river, but according to my gran, I'd lost both, so there was no way I was getting in! For much of my childhood I didn't think I was eligible for connection with God, and it wasn't until way into adulthood that I met with God for myself.

CRASHING INTO GOD

It was actually quite unceremonious circumstances that led me to Him. At that time, my life was chaotic to say the least: it was full of stress and although I was doing very well professionally and in my outer world, on the inside I was really struggling with low self-esteem, with money issues and all kinds of personal battles and identity crises.

I'd had a huge falling-out with my boyfriend, fuelled by lies told about me that hurt me deeply, and that had sent my already high stress levels through the roof. It wasn't just the situation or the lies – my *life* hurt. I was in deep emotional pain and inner turmoil and I couldn't shake it.

One day while out driving I became distracted and lost track of where I was. The traffic in front of me had stopped, but I failed to put my foot on the brakes in time and my car ran into the back of the one in front with an almighty *thud!* Something about that bump sent me into a kind of bubble, outside of which everything was moving in slow motion. I saw the driver of the car jump out of his vehicle in slow motion. I saw him running towards me in slow motion. I saw him knock on my car window, in very slow motion, and heard his words: *Are you all right?*

Inside the bubble, everything was happening in real time: the pain and the anguish were in real time, as was my desperation. I found myself thinking, *I don't want to be here. I think I want to die.* I *really* wanted to die! Thoughts of Bianca, my baby, helped me remember and realize that dying wasn't an option. *My baby needs me, my baby needs me,* I thought. And quite spontaneously, without logical thought, I found myself... well, I guess you'd call it praying: 'God,' I said on a very deep exhale, 'I really, really need you to help me. *Please* help me!'

To this day I don't remember how I got home or what happened with the cars – it was as if none of that had happened – but I know once I arrived there I went to my bed and I stayed there for three whole days. I don't remember eating, drinking or going to the loo – I broke down and I lost my composure. I had nothing left.

I've a vague recollection of my daughter putting her head around the door from time to time and asking sheepishly, 'Mum... are you all right?' It was my dark night of the soul. But, unusually for me back then, and perhaps even unconsciously, I found myself prayerful. I needed help like never before and weirdly it sent me searching for my Bible. It was weird because up to that point I'd never really tried to read a Bible, apart from in RE at school. To me, the text always seemed like a foreign language, with all those thees and thous and other complicated words; I just never managed to make sense of it.

But there I was, turning the bookshelves upside down trying to find one. Eventually I did, and I went back to bed and let the thick, dusty hardback open on a page at random. 'The Gospel According to Matthew,' I read out loud and something strange began to happen. As I read the words on the page I heard a voice within me: a man's voice. It sounded familiar, and yet I knew with certainty that I'd never heard it before. The more I read the words on the page, the louder and more real the man's voice became.

He kept saying: 'I love you. I love you, Dion. I know you don't know me, but I know you and *I love you*. I *know* you're in a mess and I can see how you got here, but I love you. I know your thinking's all jacked up, but I love you. Let *me* lead you out of the mess and the pain, because I love you. There's so much for you to do, so much for you to be. There's so much more to you than you could ever know. There's another way, another path, you're going the wrong way. I love you so much and I don't want you to go the wrong way. I want you to go the right way. Let me show you the way.'

This voice was so real to me – not in a loud, booming, fill-the-room kind of way, but in an inwardly strong and audible way – that I began to wonder if I was losing my mind. Eventually, I spoke back: 'God, is this really you?' I don't know if the yes was audible, but right there in wonderment and confusion about what I was experiencing, deep down I knew I was having a conversation with God.

Still speaking out loud, I made Him a promise: 'I'll give you three months to show me this conversation is real, that I'm not crazy. That you're real and what you say is true. I'll go to church, I'll read the Bible, I'll pray, I'll do my bit to seek you and search you out. God, I really need you to show me you're real.'

These weren't things that He asked me to do: they were things that I thought were fitting and right to do. I offered to do them with a clean heart. God honoured them, and through them our relationship began to grow. And so it was that a series of events opened up a new communication and connection between me and God. I actually spoke with God, as in having a conversation, for the first time ever, and in that conversation He spoke to me audibly and told me that He loved me and that He had a plan for my life. I was never the same after that experience, or alone. Wherever I go, God goes with me.

BRINGING HEAVEN TO THE MARKETPLACE

I recently attended a leadership training course in Wales alongside high-level leaders from various sectors. Once again, I was the only black woman in the group and also the only Christian, although spirituality was definitely not a taboo topic – there was lots of talk about fairies, unicorns, angels, the Buddha, Higher Selves and animal spirits.

In one session we were split into groups and tasked to work together as a team to 'change the world'. Of course it was a game but it had a serious objective: we were exploring leadership and our own leadership styles. As a team, we had unlimited resources and could do whatever we wanted. My group had 12 participants and it was *chaotic* – each person had made up their own mind about what should take priority and spoke with great knowledge and insight about what our steps should be.

The trouble was, in my estimation, we were nowhere near on the same page as a team. Everyone was talking over everyone else, and no one realized, or was willing to admit, that we didn't know what we were doing. Although they were clueless, each participant spoke in that heady, intelligent, certainty-laden way.

I noticed that I felt deflated and unable to compete. Usually, this would be my cue to invite God into the picture, but that wasn't going to hack it here. I wanted – in fact, I *needed*, if I was going to be able to contribute to the task – to get clear on what we did know and what we didn't; what we were certain about and what the actual problem was. I needed to sit with the problem for a bit, and to ask God to show us the way.

I tried to make up my mind whether or not I would share my honest thoughts. I realized this kind of suggestion didn't fit in at all! And right then, even though it was just an exercise in some hypothetical situation, I felt a lot like the way I'd felt many, many times before in leadership – that what I have to say, and more importantly, what God might have to say, just doesn't match the sound of what's being said.

On the one hand my faith and connection with God has been the single most powerful factor in my own transformation journey. Spiritual connection has become my superpower: I've come to understand God as the difference that makes a difference in the success of anything and everything concerning me. I've come to trust that His ways are perfect and that His guidance, mixed with my life and leadership experience and expertise, is the winning combination I know will work. But on the other hand, in this world I was feeling inept and incapable of showing up in this potent, divine power.

I trusted God and yet having Him with me was an obstacle because my relationship with Him and my devotion to Him seemed to cost me my credibility with the people I wanted to see me, hear me and take me seriously and validate me. My feeling was that they wouldn't do that if I brought my sense of God into the open. It felt like I had to choose, one or the other.

A STATE OF MIND CALLED IN-GODDEDNESS

So, obviously, since I'm writing this here in the book, I've come out of the closet with my God connection and made my choice to unapologetically connect to Him. You don't get to have me show up without my spiritual side because I'm all in with the mission to make the marketplace a fairer, more just and equal place that supports the greater good. And I'm fully persuaded that, if we're going to be successful in this mission, we need God in marketplace affairs.

I'm sharing this from my heart because it's my strongest and truest conviction. I don't want to alienate you. I don't want to make you wrong for what you believe. I don't want to push you away because of what I believe. I want you to connect with me and this book. I want you to benefit from this and I want you to grow. But I can't withhold what I know about connecting with God, such is my conviction of the power of that connection.

There's a whole movement, exacerbated by the coronavirus pandemic, about self-care and self-love, and it's born out of high stress. We've organized ourselves in such a way that we're in constant danger of burnout and breakdown. So we're on high alert, with alarms going off saying, 'Take care of yourself! You'd better love yourself. You'd better take care of yourself! Otherwise you're going to burn out.'

We acknowledge the need for self-love in the marketplace because it's a place of high competition, huge fear around being uncovered as a fraud, not being in the in-crowd, not being equal to the best of them. This is what we've created: it's a ruthless, dog-eat-dog place in which we have to prove ourselves, and that's draining and energetically expensive.

I've found that as I consciously connect with my God, there's no need to prove myself. There's no need for us to fight our brother or our sister, or make them subordinate so that we can be dominant. In God, there's complete equality. 'In-Goddedness' is the term I use to describe connection with God: it's a state of mind, accessed through consciousness, where love is sovereign and truth reigns. It's where there's no fear and love is unconditional; it's where peace isn't dependent on the circumstances. We all want this, and actually we all need this peace and sense of being loved. Almost inevitably, we go to great lengths to find it – too often outside of a relationship with God.

MASTERING OUR CONNECTION WITH GOD

You don't have to work for love in God – because you *are* loved. You don't have to prove yourself – because you *are* known. You don't have to compete – because we *all* get to win. It's a stark contradiction to the prevailing marketplace mind. Think about that for a minute. I'm convinced that we can find whatever we need when we connect with God. Everybody is equal and God is sovereign. There's no fear, and there's no need for rivalry. I'm calling this heaven, and we're being called to bring heaven to the marketplace. Just take a moment to ask yourself what the phrase 'heaven on Earth' really means to you.

In order to be able to do this, we need to find our place in God. This is what Jesus is to me. In my spiritual life, Jesus leads the way for me to ascend in consciousness. He represents the instructions, the commandments, the direction and the way into this state of consciousness where I'm equal to everyone; where I don't have to fight to prove everything; where love is available to me. I'm loved and I'm at peace, regardless of the circumstances. In this place of connection with God, there's only truth and love. There's no inequality, and there's no question of our 'enoughness'. Finding your way to In-Goddedness is the ultimate act of self-care.

Jesus represents *my* way to In-Goddedness. It's the only way I know. My encouragement is that you seek and find *your own way*. As I press into Jesus and develop and advance my spiritual intellect through His teachings, the eyes of my understanding are opening – I understand my purpose in life, my value. I'm growing in my ability to see the truth: that you're no better than me, nor I better than you, and that all I owe anyone is love.

Connection with God is changing everything about who I am as a Queen Influencer.

I know the chances are high that we don't relate to God in the same way: the likelihood is that your spiritual views differ from mine. Even if you're a Christian like me, we probably don't see things in the same way; our relationship with God isn't the same. But that's not the issue here – this isn't about what you call God or how you call on Him: it's that you *do* call, that you *do* connect and that you *commit* to developing that connection.

I don't feel any inclination or right to tell you to pray. I don't feel any inclination or right to tell you to go to church or read the Bible – I trust you'll know what to do and I honour you. But I do boldly and unapologetically implore you to consider that what we're up to here on planet Earth isn't happening in a vacuum – we're interconnected with other realms, governed by the laws of the universe, supported and influenced by the heavens. In my opinion, to ignore this is to miss out, and it's unwise.

I completely understand the impulse to leave God out. After all, we know the history; we've heard the horrendous stories of the corruption, the fallible leadership, the tyrannical oppression of the masses. We know that some of the most horrific happenings in history were a direct result of people acting in the name of religion. So I get why we say that church and state should be disconnected. But I'm asking you to consider the idea that a disregard for all things religious doesn't have to mean we throw the baby out with the bathwater. Just because we don't want religion in the marketplace, it doesn't mean we don't need God. I say we need God like never before.

SPIRITUAL INTELLIGENCE IS IMPERATIVE

I respect and honour your right to choose your own spiritual path, but I'm unapologetic about asking you to be open to the idea that connecting with God – in whatever form that takes for you – is a critical aspect of our preparation to take spiritual intelligence, spiritual development and our spiritual evolution more seriously than we're doing right now. I searched for it in that group of 12, and I've been searching for it in meetings with clients and conversations with leaders, and I find there's *so* much resistance to bringing the two together.

As I said earlier, I believe that we're spirit beings who have a soul and live in a body having a human experience – we are *spirit* and yet this spiritual aspect of ourselves appears to be taboo and denied at the heart of the marketplace king, particularly in the realm of senior leadership. In her brilliant talk 'Holy Language' author Caroline Myss describes this 'phenomenon of our times' as a 'repelling of the sacred'. She says that in unprecedented ways, we've shut God out of our lives, and to such an extent that we're now the only society ever to have lived and led in an atmosphere that questions His very existence.

Never before has it been more likely that mentioning God will bring about disdain and repulsion, rather than acknowledgement that God in some shape or form is real. I see and hear the evidence of this on a daily basis. In my experience and through my eyes, it's not that we don't worship or think of God in the same way; it's not a problem that we don't have the same words, rituals and practices. Our differences are not the problem: it's more that most people I meet and work with are only *superficially* connected to the God they say they're connected to.

In reality, they're nominal, on the fence, disengaged, and they lack commitment of any real depth to their own self-confessed spiritual belief system. Their belief system isn't challenging their growth, their leadership or their conscience in any real or evolutionary way; their relationship with their God doesn't challenge them to show up, or to address marketplace difficulties from a spiritual place.

We don't see our spirituality as appropriate in our work life, in the business world or in the affairs of mankind. So the king, that system of which we're all a part, isn't influenced by God and can therefore continue to perpetuate unequal, unrighteous, unjust and unfair results without divine challenge or accountability.

God has been edged out completely. We lead from our heads, from our logic, from our IQ. The king excels in the use of our intelligence quotient, or IQ: the measure of how well we think and analyse thoughts. Over the last 20 years, the movement to support the global workforce to enhance its EQ, or emotional intelligence – the measure of how well we understand what and how we feel – has gathered some momentum.

But SQ, or spiritual intelligence, which is about understanding our spiritual identity and purpose, is still largely ignored. SQ drives delivery of our purpose for being on the planet, in this country, in this city, in this industry and organization. SQ measures how well we understand *who* we are and *why* we exist, in relation to God and everyone and everything in the universe, and it's still awkward and out of place in marketplace conversations. The lack of quality thinking around questions such as these is at the root of work–life issues. Many of us have simply not engaged in this line of enquiry – we haven't thought about it and traditional leadership training doesn't usually require us to.

IQ on its own, or even IQ and EQ together, are incomplete without SQ; in the same way that a two-legged stool cannot stand, IQ and EQ must be complemented by the spiritual aspect of our intelligence.

UNDERSTANDING THE RULES OF ENGAGEMENT

God, in whatever form we find our spiritual connection, informs the health of our world and our marketplace. God is Love and our hearts are wired to respond to this love. We need it to thrive. God speaks time and time again throughout the scriptures of His loving nature: 'I've loved you with an everlasting love; I've drawn you with loving kindness.'

God is Light – His way, His wisdom, and His word have the effect of bringing light. I can see things now that I was once blind to: things that were fuzzy and unclear became focused and laser sharp. When I can't see the way forward or what to do next, or when things seem dark, I remind myself that God is our light. He reveals answers and makes solutions visible.

God is omniscient – He knows everything. God transforms – He changes people and situations beyond recognition. When I think back to the woman I was when I crashed my car or the life I led when I lived behind the mask; when I consider the type of leader I was, struggling with imposter syndrome and paralysed with the fear that the racist narrative I'd grown up hearing was true about me. When I think of it all, I see the evidence of God's power to transform lives and situations. God *directs* – as a shepherd directs sheep. He leads and His way is always perfect.

When we don't prioritize and take seriously our connection with God, we don't know what we're missing out on and we don't know what we don't know. We don't know what's available to us. We don't know the difference that God can make in our day-to-day living and leadership and our day-to-day mission to influence the king.

About a year ago, while engaging in some Bible study, I looked at the story of one of the prophets, Jeremiah, who was having a conversation with God (actually, a very similar conversation to the one I'd had with God after the car cash). God was telling Jeremiah that He was calling him to go to the nations. I imagined the conversation: 'I'm going to send you to speak My word,' said God. 'I'm going to send you to proclaim My will. I'm going to send you to help people understand what they should do. I want you to bring my ideas and bring my admonishments, bring my declarations and decrees to the people.'

But Jeremiah, being a young boy, was a bit intimidated by all that God had in store for him. He asked Him: 'Are you sure you've got the right guy, God?' He could think of so many reasons why he wasn't qualified for the job. 'I'm young, so they won't listen to me. I'm not influential enough. I haven't got what it takes. I'm not qualified.'

And God said: 'Don't tell me how old you are, Jeremiah. Remember, I'm the one who made you – you come from me! I know who you are. I know where you are and still I say this is my purpose for your life!'

I'd read this scripture a million times before but I'd never seen it in quite this way. God said: 'Before you were in your mother's womb, I knew you.' It struck me like lightning: before Jeremiah was conceived, he existed! Before he was here, he was there. With God. Before he was born he was alive and purposed and destined for his earthly purpose in God. All of a sudden the heavens opened up and I was captivated by the thought that if Jeremiah was with God before he was born, before he came to Earth, *what else* is with God? What else is there that needs to be here?

My imagination was ablaze! I wondered if the answers to hard questions are with God. Well, I already knew the answer to that: I'd been receiving answers to my hard questions throughout my relationship with Him. But what if new insights and new ideas and new solutions were with God *before* they were here? What if all that we need to do, all that we dream of doing, is just waiting in God to get to us right now?

I wondered, was the Internet available on Earth during the Stone Age? Was the understanding that the Earth is a globe available when the prevailing belief was that it was flat? Do there exist, right now, the answers to the question of how we can squash inequality in the education system across the globe? Or how racism can be annihilated once and for all? Or how we can heal rifts between nations or transform marketplace systems and restore equality, justice and fairness among us?

One of the things that being a Christian gives me – something I see is missing in the lives and leadership of many of the women I support, who don't have a formal belief system – is an understanding of the rules of engagement. By that, I mean understanding how to access and maximize God's power and support. The Bible spells out how God is asking to be approached and what's required for the relationship to work, and this kind of information and understanding is as important in connecting with God as it is in any relationship.

I think of it like this… Electricity is a powerful form of energy, and that energy can cook your dinner or it can cook you; that energy can warm your home on a cold winter's night or it can burn your house to the ground on that same night! The difference in outcomes lies in how you engage with electricity: it works *if* you put the right plug in the right socket; it doesn't work well if you take your hairdryer into the bath with you. There are rules of engagement to maximize the benefits of electricity.

If we're to take connecting with God seriously – if we accept that this divine exchange is available to us – we each and collectively need to put thought into working out how we think that can happen. What are the rules of engagement? The more I think about this the more I'm persuaded the answers exist in God; and the way we access what's in God is through intimacy with God. I believe that we must connect with God and make room for him in our leadership. God wants to help us – we were never supposed to figure it all out by ourselves, without Him. We're wired for connection with Him.

GOD CARES ABOUT INEQUALITY

In Matthew 25: 34–45, Jesus teaches that a day is coming when the King of Kings will gather the nations and say: 'Come, you who are blessed by my Father; take your inheritance, the kingdom prepared for you since the creation of the world. For I was hungry and you gave me something to eat, I was thirsty and you gave me something to drink, I was a stranger and you invited me in, I needed clothes and you clothed me, I was sick and you looked after me, I was in prison and you came to visit me.

'Then the righteous will answer him, "Lord, when did we see you hungry and feed you, or thirsty and give you something to drink? When did we see you a stranger and invite you in, or needing clothes and clothe you? When did we see you sick or in prison and go to visit you?"

'The King will reply, "Truly I tell you, whatever you did for one of the least of these brothers and sisters of mine, you did for me."

'Then he will say to those on his left, "Depart from me, you who are cursed, into the eternal fire prepared for the devil and his angels. For I was hungry and you gave me nothing to eat, I was thirsty and you gave me nothing to drink, I was a stranger and you did not invite me in, I needed clothes and you did not clothe me, I was sick and in prison and you did not look after me."

'They also will answer, "Lord, when did we see you hungry or thirsty or a stranger or needing clothes or sick or in prison, and did not help you?"

'He will reply, "Truly I tell you, whatever you did not do for one of the least of these, you did not do for me."'

God cares about inequality.

Mastering our connection with God is as much a part of leadership strategy as networking or assertive communication skills. If we shore up our standing in God – if we go all in, learn the rules of engagement, do what needs to be done to maximize the connection – my conviction is that as we seek God, we will find him, because He seeks us. He has a vested interest in our success and leadership in the global marketplace.

Who is your God? What is your Higher Power? What does reconnecting with your God and your spirit mean to you? How would you show up differently in the marketplace if you brought your God with you? What is your God saying about inequality in your industry, your organization, your world, and your role in it?

RECLAIMING WHOLENESS

The dictionary defines wholeness as the state of being unbroken and undamaged. I know from experience that as achieving women – women who climb the marketplace ladders and accomplish a high level of success at work – we don't tend to walk around saying to ourselves *I'm broken* or *I'm damaged*.

In fact, I remember the red-hot anger on the face of one client when I asked her to examine more deeply the huge resentment she harboured towards a male colleague. 'I'm sick of being told that I'm the one who needs to be fixed!' she screamed at me. 'Why can't *he* be the one who's told to change his ways?'

She's not the only woman who feels this way. I'm hearing this sentiment everywhere I go: 'Women don't need to be fixed!' It's usually a rebuttal to the misconceived notion that if women would only use a different tone of voice, or find their forceful side, or learn to be like this or that, *then* they'd have a chance at equality and *then* they'd experience greater leadership success.

The idea that women need to 'fixed' before we're worthy of equal pay, access, treatment or opportunities is both irritating and plain wrong; especially when being 'fixed' means becoming more like professional men. Women *don't need to be fixed*, and we're *already* equal to men!

SINGING THE SONG OF WHOLENESS

All this said, I believe that what we *do* need is to reclaim and re-establish wholeness; in other words, we must *heal ourselves*. For me, the reclamation of wholeness is synonymous with establishing wellness. This is a massive topic, worthy of a book in its own right; indeed, as early as the 4th century BC the Greek philosopher Socrates wrote about the importance of wholeness and warned against treating one part of the body while ignoring the interconnectedness of all other parts of the person.

So, wholeness is about the interconnectedness and harmonious alignment of the different aspects of our being – mind, body, spirit and soul. When I think of how Carl Jung defined wholeness – as the state in which the conscious mind and the unconscious mind work together in *harmony* – in my mind's eye I see a band in which body, mind, soul and spirit are singing in their own unique tone, all singing in harmony and together creating a melody. For me, wholeness is the condition we reach when all of these aspects of our being are singing what I call the 'song of wholeness':

I'm safe, I matter, I have value, I belong here, I'm loved,
I'm whole, I'm well,
All is well with me.

146

If it's this unified sentiment that manifests wholeness, I have to tell you that in my experience of working behind the mask with women leaders, far too many of them are leading in a way that's inconsistent with wholeness and experiencing varying degrees of brokenness.

Though some of these women appear to be the picture of wellness *physically* – suited and booted in the finest clothes and sporting expensive haircuts and delicately manicured hands – at the same time, they are secretly tearing themselves down with negative self-talk. I've seen the most confident, vocal, opinionated leaders battle with physical pain, suffering from arthritis, multiple sclerosis or some other chronic disease. I've seen self-confessed great leaders with important things to say cower in meetings because they feel their views will put them in danger somehow. This mismatch, this out-of-alignment-ness, is perhaps more prevalent than you might imagine.

What I find is that when wholeness is undermined, when harmony between mind, body, soul and spirit is disrupted, it almost invariably started with words – a narrative or a story, either self-devised or taught to us by others. Words can affect and infect our mind, body, soul and spirit with bitterness, resentment, shame or guilt – often without our awareness and often in ways we underestimate. We're oblivious of the extent to which words affect us and our leadership. I've been learning this lesson in very personal and powerful ways...

UNCOVERING MY TRUTH

I've always known I'm great. I've never really struggled to admit or accept this about myself in a logical, matter-of-fact way. I did well at school, passed my exams, and went to university. You know, I can think for myself, and I can understand complex things. I've always known this about myself. Plus, I've always held a sense of pre-destined greatness – as if I was born to do something significant and important in the world.

On some levels I sang the wholeness song with conviction, passion even. I'm guessing you do too. This knowing isn't rare among us women who lead; in fact, I don't think we could be where we are today, leading within our organizations, industries and fields, if at some level we didn't think this way about ourselves. And yet for me, in other ways this conviction couldn't have seemed more untrue.

This really landed front of mind when one of my social media associates shared that she was about to publish a book. From what she was saying, the book would be a controversial one that would rock boats and ruffle feathers. She didn't let on what it was about, but she explained that its message was one she felt she'd been born to bring to the spotlight. She said that for many years she'd been trying to escape it because she didn't want to accept the call to provoke the discussion the book would initiate, and she confessed she was nervous about how the book and its message would be received.

At that time, I was really finding my own voice and understanding the call on my own life to support women to show up, speak up and shake things up more influentially. So I was both excited for my 'friend' and also really aware of how scary and challenging this could be for her. I reached out and told her how proud I was that she was taking a stand. I told her that, even though I didn't yet know what her message was, I knew in my heart that her courage in sharing it would be good for our world in some way.

I told her that I would make myself available to her if things got tough – if she ever needed a safe place to talk, cry, remember, re-ground in her motives for sharing her message. I meant it because I know the kind of pressure that's possible when you dare to call things out and expose things that others would prefer stayed hidden.

The book was about racism, in particular the role of white women in the perpetuation of racism! OMG! I'd never heard anything like this expressed in writing, and it changed my life in more ways than one. The biggest change was my reaction to the woman who'd written the book. In my opinion, her writing was *so* angry, and I felt that the way she'd explained herself and shared her message in videos and articles after the book's release, and the way she'd responded to comments and questions about her work, was plain rude, even aggressive.

I thought she'd made some very valid points, but I'd go so far as to say I hated her delivery of them. Since I'd offered to be an ally she reached out to me and asked me to comment and support one of her posts. When I read it, I felt regret that I'd ever offered my support to this woman. I felt I couldn't, shouldn't, wouldn't condone what I read as an ungracious attack on white women. I'm a black woman too, I thought, but I just don't feel the way you do! Your experience doesn't mirror mine.

I felt so conflicted, so bad that I'd promised support I no longer wanted to give. I knew I needed to talk with her and that I had to be honest. We had a challenging conversation, during which she told me she didn't need my permission or support to say what she was saying in the way she was saying it. I completely agreed with that, but things were never the same between us afterwards, and some time later I noticed I'd been blocked from her social media platform. I was sad about that, but some good came out of this for me.

I couldn't rest after we'd spoken; for days the whole thing felt unfinished for me. I couldn't put my finger on exactly what was bothering me so much, but in the end it boiled down to this question: I don't feel the same way as this black woman – I don't share her anger and aggression and I don't want to be rude or disrespectful to white people – but what *do* I think? Where *do* I stand on this issue of black and whiteness? I couldn't answer the question and it plagued me. I prayed: 'God, what's really going on here? Why is this hurting and tormenting me so? Help me see the truth.'

One night I dreamed I was locked in a cold and sparse prison cell. I became aware of footsteps on the concrete floor of the prison corridor and the jangling of keys in the hands of a guard. Soon I could see the guard – a giant white man with a massive beer belly, dressed in a sheriff's uniform, hat n' all.

When he was stood almost outside my cell I called to the guard: 'I want to get out of here. I want to go there.' I pointed to a building in the distance, on the other side of the prison courtyard, that we could both see through a window. It was a magnificent palace that was hosting a grand ball. I could see dancing and merriment and opulence; I could see beautiful gowns and hear wonderful music as if played by a fine orchestra. 'Over there' was vibrant and full of colour and elegance and splendour.

'I want to go there,' I said again to my big-bellied steward. He cocked his head to one side and gave me a blank, cold stare. I couldn't even tell if he'd heard me. He fiddled thoughtfully with the huge bunch of keys that jangled in his hand and then in a tone that was as unemotional as the way he'd looked at me, he said: 'I'll let you out of here, but I'll be damned if I'm going to let you in there.' He pointed in the direction of the palace. As he opened the door of the prison cell, I woke up.

That dream felt *so* real to me that I lay in bed for several moments before making any kind of move to start my day. 'What was that, God?' I whispered in prayer. Over the next couple of days my understanding of the dream's significance began to unfold with alarming clarity. I saw how I held deep within me the belief that the white man had the keys; the white man had the power to lock me up and release me; the white man decided where I could go and where I couldn't; the white man decided whether or not I could go to the ball. People like me are slaves at the mercy of the white masters!

I have goose bumps as I share this with you now, and on my development journey this question of how someone with such a sense of greatness, value and destiny can simultaneously see herself as a slave girl in a jail cell has been a recurring one. It doesn't make sense. It's not aligned. It doesn't equal wholeness.

A QUEEN INFLUENCER'S DEFENCE STRATEGY

Over the years I've seen that I'm not the only one whose wholeness has been undermined by words, lies, messages, pronouncements, decrees and declarations. Who said it, why they said it, what they meant when they said it and what we made it mean when it was said are, of course, different and unique for each woman.

However, it feels as if I've heard it all: some women suffered at the hands of a wicked parent; some were raped or sexually abused; some were bullied badly at school; others were born 'too' something or other, like the many clients born too dark-skinned for their parents' liking. The women I coach tell me their version of the story around too-much-mouth-ness. I definitely identify with this one – more often than not, when we're branded mouthy at a young age it has more to do with *what* we have to say than the fact that we said it. We got people's backs up – we saw and spoke things that people didn't want to hear.

Some of my clients have received inexplicable diagnoses of mysterious, incurable, psychosomatic 'syndromes' that mean they will never be quite 'normal'. One told me the story of how she was born a girl when both her parents badly wanted a boy. Another survived her mother's attempt to abort her – by the time everyone realized the abortion had failed, it was too late and 'they were stuck with' her.

Some women were commanded to live up to some superior ideal far removed from who they actually are; some were given names that would serve as official decrees of their destiny: one explained that her name meant 'frail'. Others tell their own version of abandonment or betrayal: an infidelity, a failed marriage, estranged children who want nothing to do with their own mother.

It's as though each one of us, in our own unique way, has experienced the same violent, invisible attack on our ability to sing the wholeness song. It's as though dark, mysterious forces have conspired to kill off the sense of our own greatness and, along with that, our potential. It's as though wickedness is gathering its troops in a dedicated mission to quash the soul of womanity and her sense of wholeness. Sometimes even before we've begun to formulate a sense of who we are; sometimes before we're even born, and at other times as we grow on our journey to young womanhood.

For me, it almost always comes as a surprise when skilful coaching questions bring these stories to the fore. Some clients say things like, 'That's all in the past,' or 'I'm over that now,' or 'That was then, this is now.' Their instincts tell them to leave a particular issue alone, that there's no reason to open that can of worms. My response is always the same: if it's coming up in this conversation about what's happening with you at work right now, it's definitely an issue and there's definitely a good reason to open it up and take a look.

If our old wounds stay unresolved and unhealed, if historical bitterness, resentment, shame, guilt or the inability to forgive roam free and unchallenged within us, they fracture the harmony and break the wholeness that helps us to withstand the challenges that we are bound to encounter as our relationship with the king evolves. Leading without wholeness is too often hazardous to women's wellbeing.

I think of reclaiming wholeness as the influencer's defence strategy and the edge that helps us thrive through the ups and downs associated with being and becoming more influential. By its very nature, this new dimension of leadership and sovereign influence we're growing into requires us to take off our masks, break cover, stand in the firing line and make ourselves vulnerable. In order to influence people we need to show ourselves, and invariably this comes with the risk of being shot down, misunderstood, targeted, undermined, overlooked, or all of the above.

We can expect to be rejected, dismissed, or even ridiculed when presenting new ideas that go against the grain. The women leaders who can stand despite this, those who can stay the course and genuinely thrive and maintain wellness – without breaking down, burning out and backing off, and without sabotaging their health, energy, enthusiasm, ethics and self-esteem – are making a conscious habit of reclaiming and establishing their wholeness.

DO YOU WANT TO BE HEALED?

The Bible tells story after story of men and women who came to Jesus for healing. Over and over again Jesus would ask the same question: 'Do you want to be healed?' 'Do you want to be made whole?' At first I felt this was inappropriate. I'd think to myself, why would you ask that, Jesus? Of course they want to be healed. Isn't this obvious?

As I travel on my own path to wholeness, and as I come alongside my clients, I've learned that there are 'benefits' to holding on to our old, unresolved stuff. For some of us, this looks like retaining the right to blame; for others it means not having to face responsibilities or to venture beyond the comfort zone.

We each have to decide for ourselves that we can't stay like this any more – we have to decide it's time to be made whole, to regain our capacity to move, shift, advance, change, grow, evolve, mature and move on from the experiences and the chains of our past. I've faced this question many times on my ongoing journey to wholeness and I know that responding to it positively will challenge me to confront hard things within me.

Old offences, resentments, bitterness and unforgiveness – these things can't go with us into the new dimension of influence we're being called to. They're like shackles that bind our movement and cause us to stumble on the road towards our own influential becoming. We must seek to forgive, to find new ways of seeing what we've been through. We must confront those parts of ourselves that insist on holding on to the pain, the lies and the conclusions we've drawn from past events and become masters of releasing and letting go. If you have unacknowledged feelings of rage, your leadership and your decision to grow will give them a platform where they can demand to be taken seriously.

I know that feelings, especially those we have at work, can be tricky. They seem like a can of worms and there can be tremendous fear around what will happen if you open that up, if you open yourself up to letting your feelings surface. But the truth is that feeling isn't a struggle; trying *not* to feel is the struggle. Fighting to ignore your feelings is the struggle. Forcing yourself to go on as if your feelings don't exist is the struggle.

This is why I say you should acknowledge and welcome your feelings as a messenger bearing gifts. Resist the urge to suppress, depress and tear down your feelings. Stop, connect, allow and listen for the message your feelings have come to deliver. See what your feelings have come to reveal to you about the state of your soul and the needs of your heart.

Allowing yourself to feel, see, confront, face and revisit yesterday's trauma or pain is a powerful part of pursuing wholeness. I promise you that you'll come through to the other side. Be kind to yourself – being strong isn't the same as being unfeeling or in denial. You don't have to be tough as old boots and hard as nails, Influential Woman! Don't be afraid. Make room, feel, be unbothered by other people's opinions, and be made whole.

It took a Facebook 'friend' writing a book that horrified me and a dream about a jail to show me that deep and dark beliefs, and bitterness and resentment that I really didn't know I held, were undermining my wholeness. I can tell you that facing those thoughts and accepting them as my own took everything. And keeping those thoughts from re-establishing themselves in my heart, mind, soul and spirit takes work – daily, ongoing work.

I sought the best support and allowed myself to face it all because I understand the power of pursuing and reclaiming wholeness. One day, at the height of my despair, I wrote a letter titled 'Dear White Women'. You don't need to know what I poured out onto those pages, but I do want you to know how, with each word, the walls that stood to divide my inner wholeness came tumbling down. I want you to know how freeing it was to purge myself of thoughts and hurts and memories – some of which I'm convinced weren't even my own but had been passed down through the generations.

I want you to know how powerful the results have been: at one time, rejection, criticism and misunderstandings regularly incapacitated me and derailed me from my purpose, but now I use them as fuel to keep going and as opportunities for growth. I'm able to do this directly because of the work I've committed to around reclaiming my wholeness and embodying the queenly influence to which I've been called.

START WITH THE PAIN

There are many ways to approach freeing yourself from the things that threaten your wholeness. You can write a letter, like I did, or you can work with a coach or talk to a therapist. I can't stress enough how powerful this process is – sometimes it's really hard to see from a new perspective by yourself. But if you choose to, you can spend time in meditation or contemplation, or try journalling and working through some questions on your own.

The advice I give all my clients is to start where pain or conflict or hurt are showing up now. Delving into your thoughts behind these will take you powerfully to where there's unresolved brokenness from the past. Thinking about the thoughts that cause you pain shows you where greater healing still needs to take place. As a way of making a start, you can ask yourself the following questions:

- Who/what hurt you?

- What do you wish you'd said to them?

- What are you angry about? What are you sad about?

- What are the recurring challenges and themes here?

- What are the things that trigger you about this?

- Why are you feeling/thinking/behaving in this way?

- When was the first time you felt like this?

HABIT #5

REFRAMING

Have you heard the expression winners never quit and quitters never win? Years ago, I had a mentor who would almost sing these words to me every time I met with him. But here's the thing – they're not true! Through experience, I've discovered that sometimes the wisest thing to do is get the hell out, throw in the towel, or walk away.

A big part of what I do with my private clients is help them make decisions about when to quit and when to stay, fight through, or endure the process. More often than not, the urge to quit comes when things are hard, painful, heavy, stressful – and as a woman in leadership you'll know there'll be no shortage of all of the above as we set out to lead change that truly matters.

So, if you want to stay on the path to ascension as a Queen Influencer and resist the urge to quit when the going gets tough, this next habit is a game changer. Reframing: finding new ways to see your situation and better ways to look at what you're going through.

REFRAMING GRAN'S PICTURE

I learned the term 'reframe' when I was studying to become a Master Practitioner of Neuro-Linguistic Programming (NLP), but it was an old picture owned by my grandmother that really helped me understand the power of this process.

Over the years my gran and I have argued playfully about her attachment to what in my eyes is old tat but to her is fondly cherished antiques – let's just say we have very different tastes. One such object was a picture of a boy and his dog that had pride of place over the mantelpiece in her living room. I don't know who the artist was, but to say I disliked his work is putting it mildly. The painting was dark, bland and sombre, and my gran loved it.

A while ago, during a bout of spring-cleaning, I managed quite by accident to knock the painting off the wall. It bounced as it hit the floor, and I heard a loud crack. On inspecting it I saw that miraculously it was intact, but the frame had broken in several places. My gran was visibly upset, but I reassured her: 'Don't worry, I'll get it reframed.'

A few weeks later, while I was at work, my dad rehung the newly framed painting in its place of prominence. When I walked into the room later that day, the first thing I noticed was the picture, and it took my breath away. It looked so different, and much to my surprise, I actually liked it a lot! Setting it in a more contemporary frame had made all the difference. In fact, it looked like a completely new piece – it really struck me, the difference this reframing had made.

REFRAMING THE PRESSURE

In the years since I first encountered the principle of reframing, I've seen just how powerful it can be in leadership to master the art of reframing whatever it is that you're going through at work in order to see it from a new perspective. As women and as leaders, reframing is an essential skill for finding growth and truth in our challenges. In this chapter I want to share with you a few examples of the reframes that you'll find useful and applicable, despite what you go through on the journey to influencing the king.

As we discussed in Chapter 3, pressure is inevitable: the pressure of the times, the pressure of the prevailing power structures and the hierarchy within which we lead, and the pressure from within. Many of the women I meet, including myself, have felt at some point that the weight of the pressure is too much to bear, as if they're buckling under it.

Sometimes when I listen to women describing how they can feel surrounded by it all, it's as if womanity is at the intersection of these three pressures. It reminds me of a baby in the womb – in my mind's eye, I see a picture of womanity surrounded by these muscular walls of pressure, pressing and pushing and squeezing us. It's uncomfortable.

But what if the pressure were *advancing* us? What if the pressure were exactly what we need to help us stir the dormant yet unexpressed greatness and power within us? What if the pressure could become the perfect guide to move us – like the womb moves the baby – showing us the way to a new dimension of influence at such a time as this?

As I shared in the Introduction, I went through a great deal of pressure while writing this book. At times I felt crushed by the weight of it all. I experienced the waves of pressure as spiritual and emotional pain; it hurt so much when it felt as if I wouldn't be able to express myself and that the book wasn't working. It felt like physical pain.

At the height of the pressure, my instinct was to run, quit, throw in the towel. But the pressure of a fast-approaching deadline wouldn't let me quit; the pressure wouldn't let me back away when I made myself reframe the doubts and fears and call it what it really was: the force behind my *becoming*.

Because pressure isn't here to hurt us – it's here to move us. As evolving Queen Influencers, called to accept our co-mission with the king, we must learn how to change the way we see the pressure and master the art of letting the pressure guide us.

I can't help but see the parallel between this and the birth experience of both mother and baby in the womb – each is guided so powerfully by pressure. When the pressure of the contraction comes, the mother will experience an overwhelming urge to bear down and push, and the baby will have no choice but to move in the direction of the force. Sometimes it will restrict the oxygen supply to the baby – the baby's heart rate and heartbeat pattern will have to change to compensate for the reduction in circulating oxygen because of the pressure. I felt exactly that when I became a mother…

'Let the pressure guide you,' said Nancy, my midwife. All of a sudden I'd become aware of what felt like a solid, rock-hard ball of fire deep and low within my core. It took my breath away. It felt like a golf ball advancing downwards from the pit of my being; one minute it wasn't there, the next it dominated my consciousness without apology and it was expanding by the second, demanding I expand along with it. 'That's the baby's head,' Nancy explained. I could hardly take it in. The pressure was unlike anything I'd ever known: it was real and it was *unrelenting*.

Later, after the millionth retelling of the gory details of my baby's birth to the family and friends who poured into the hospital to meet our new arrival, I found myself wondering how Nancy had known it was time for me to push. I'd been labouring for hours prior to that, but she'd obviously seen something on my face or in my demeanour or heard something shift in the visceral groans that were involuntarily emitted from my belly and out through my mouth. She'd known the time had come for me to shift gear, sit up, pay attention and push because I was about to become a mum!

I wasn't a midwife back then, but I went on to become one, and I've lost count of the number of times I've given the same direction to the labouring women who were in my charge over the years. They'd say, 'I don't know what to do! I'm dying! I'm not going to make it. I can't do this!' and I'd whisper in their ear, 'Let the pressure guide you.'

The birthing analogy really works for me. When the pressure hits, I visualize myself being birthed to the platform that enables me to touch more lives and make my influential mark – to transform womanity and expand her power to influence the king. I held these thoughts when the pressure hit; I breathed them in as if they were pain relief.

This is what it's like to reframe. Sometimes we recite affirmations with joy in our souls and peace in our hearts, other times we barely scrape through, reframing by the skin of our teeth. Either way, reframing what you're going through is a game-changing habit that can make all the difference during the trials of leadership.

REFRAMING THE SHIT

'We're going through too much shit!' I don't mean to offend you with this turn of phrase – I'm not the type to hurl expletives around just for effect – but honestly, I can't tell you how regularly I hear this word used to describe the real work experiences of many of the women I serve. These are great women, smart women, senior leading women from every culture, creed, belief system and religion; women who lead in public and private sectors, junior managers and senior execs alike.

Even women who don't usually swear or hate swearing have exclaimed this same sentiment to me over and over, in a variety of ways. When feelings are running high, when guards are down, when emotions are charged and, on more than a few occasions, when tears are flowing, they say: 'I'm in the middle of so much shit'; 'I'm drowning in shit'; 'This place is full of shit'; or 'The shit's about to hit the fan.'

I really saw the prevalence of this after I posted one of my articles in a couple of groups on LinkedIn. It got a buzzing response: women around the world reported on their professional reality – what they were going through as Women of Influence and contemporary leaders. But it was what one woman wrote in a private message to me that really caught my attention: 'Dion, you wouldn't believe the amount of shit we're having to deal with right now, and it stinks to high heaven!' It made me smile because I knew exactly what she was talking about.

I remember where I was working when I first noticed leaders talking about 'all the shit' they were having to deal with. I'd been appointed as the resident executive coach in a firm that was going through major challenges and was at risk of failing to meet industry standards. I was given an office and the staff were asked to book themselves in on a voluntary basis to meet with me. Everyone was surprised by how many sessions were booked and during meetings one word kept coming up time after time – all the *shit*.

FROM SHIT TO MANURE

During one session a woman said to me: 'You don't know all the shit that's going on here!' In that moment the heavens opened up and I realized that what she was really saying was: 'I'm **S**cared! They're **H**olding me back! This **I**rritates me. I feel **T**hreatened, I'm in **T**rouble, and this is a **T**rial!' So SHIT became an acronym, and I realized that we need to find new, more effective ways to deal with all this mess. When women talk about the shit this is what they're really describing:

S – Scary situations

H – Hindrances, obstacles, blocks and pushbacks

I – Irritation and irritating people

T – Threats, trouble, tests, turbulence, trials

Okay, time for a reframe: it's not shit, it's *manure*! It's the thing that's going to help you grow because it contains all the nutrients you need. It stinks and it's horrible to have on you, but it's going to produce a greater leader. It's going to transform your leadership. It's going to transform your capacity to be in this place and do the work you're here to do.

As any agriculturist will tell you, manure contributes to the fertility of the soil, adding the elements necessary for whatever's planted in it to mature and thrive. I'm suggesting that all that stuff you're dealing with at work has the potential to act like manure: it has exactly the right elements and nutrients to feed your ongoing development as an influencer.

You don't have to like it or languish in it, but if you reframe it in the right way, what felt as if it could kill you can transmute as if by magic into what makes you stronger as a woman, an influencer and a change-maker – you can most certainly *grow* through it! Think about that for a minute. I want to encourage you to reframe. What if your professional struggle were a gift or an opportunity to develop as the influencer you're in your leadership role to become? What follows is an example of this.

Reframing Our Trials

One of the attendees at my most recent Leader's Lounge was a senior leader in health and social care who was on the brink of leaving her job; in fact, she'd already checked out emotionally from it months before she got to the Lounge.

Three years previously, she'd made a mistake that'd had serious implications for the organization. She'd survived the disciplinary process and was allowed to stay in her role as part of the senior leadership team, but she felt that certain colleagues weren't prepared to let her get over what had happened. She described much tension between herself and some of her colleagues, as well as lots of game playing and undercover battling, and this was all making her working life a nightmare.

The workplace had become a battleground for this woman and she found herself going on the defensive from the moment she stepped through the door. The situation was taking its toll on her health, but she struggled with it in secret, feeling the need to pretend and act as if she were 'fine'.

As she worked this through with me and the small group of women in the Lounge, she was supported and challenged to reframe and find new ways to see and interpret her experience. She thought this situation was squeezing the life out of her, so as a group we looked for new perspectives on how it could be an opportunity for her growth.

Courageously, she expanded her willingness to lay down the story of victimhood she'd been rehearsing and with new curiosity, face who she was being and how she was showing up in the situation; and how she herself was complicit in co-creating the struggle. She'd completely disconnected from her true self – she'd stopped thinking about who she was, why she was in that role, what she was there to offer, and what she could bring to the table – and instead was consumed with thoughts about what everyone else thought about her, who was saying what, who liked her and who didn't.

And she got her gold! At one point during our second day together she blurted out, 'Oh my God! I've stopped being me! I'm showing up like some scared rat – and I'm *not* a rat!' We all laughed out loud when she said this, but we knew something profound had shifted in her and that she'd never be the same at work again. With a change in perception and a powerful reframe, the whole thing had become an invitation for this brilliant Influential Woman to reconnect with her value in the organization and grow in her capacity to communicate her worth to the sceptics and naysayers.

All of a sudden this had become a development opportunity. 'I've never liked blowing my own trumpet,' the woman admitted, 'but it looks like it's time for me to make a start. I *belong* there!' We all cheered: 'Yes! You're the woman for the job – now you just need to help them see that.'

So, what scary, hindering, irritating or threatening trials are you facing at work – or at home for that matter? From this day onwards, consider reframing them to see them as the perfect conditions for your evolution as an influencer – and respond to them as such. Every situation, conflict, challenge and difficulty comes not *at* us but *for* us; it comes not to kill off our leadership impact but to help us evolve as leaders who'll influence the king.

Reframing Victim to Victor

Recently, one of my business sisters, Marianne, told me that she'd been having major success as a direct result of some of her newer connections and relationships, which had come from her networking efforts. I've long realized the potential of networking for growing a business and I really want to take my business (and influence) to a new level, so I knew it was time to step up my own networking activity.

The enthusiastic starter that I am meant I quickly began scanning networking events taking place in London and further afield and renewed my focus on creating new connections. In no time I'd secured my place at two events, and in the run-up to them I psyched myself up, gave my introverted side a good talking-to and started looking forward to hanging out and making business friends with other brilliant Women of Influence.

It turned out that I didn't enjoy the events as much as I thought I would. As I made my way home after the second one, my daughter called me because she knew how excited I'd been about going. 'Well?' she asked, with playful anticipation. 'How was it?' As I opened my mouth I heard what my daughter apparently heard too: 'It was fine. I mean, it was good...' I muttered. Who was I trying to kid? I wasn't excited and I wasn't animated; in fact, I'd found the whole experience decidedly lacklustre.

I couldn't put my finger on what was wrong, but I realized that I'd felt the same way earlier in the week after leaving the first event. Something was bothering me. I spoke to myself as I sat on the train home: *Those aren't your people. Just keep going – you'll find where you belong soon.* It wasn't until the following morning that the fog cleared and I could see where the problem lay. Let me explain what had happened.

At the first event I was asked how I was getting on with my current project. I explained the struggle and challenge I was genuinely experiencing. At the second event, I was asked about myself: who I am and how I got there. I shared bits of my journey – how I'd been working to heal shame and identity crisis in order to evolve as the woman leader and change-maker I am today.

At both events I received what felt to me like sickly pats on the shoulder. The heartfelt 'Aaawww! Oh, honey!' The other women felt sorry for me: they pitied me and their response was one of sympathy. And it *pissed me off*!

I'd been honest about the journey and the challenges and the resistance I've experienced and it was as if my sharing that had made me plummet in the eyes of those women – I'd gone from being a new business acquaintance to a poor unfortunate little bubba who's fallen over and scuffed her knees and needs comforting and consoling. *That's* the response that got my back up. It felt so inappropriate and it ignited the compulsion to fight or get the hell out of there! I shook my head and whispered to myself: *I don't want to be pitied! I want to be celebrated! I don't want to be soothed: I want to be encouraged and acknowledged as an evolving, maturing woman of power and victory!*

In the grand scheme of things those networking events weren't a big deal. The responses I'd received had just triggered old stuff in me: in a complicated, mixed-up, illogical way I'd reconnected to old self-pity and old inadequacies, and once I saw this I could handle it and quickly move on. But what did stay with me was a fresh awareness of the way we as women frame the inevitable pain and pressure that goes hand in hand with the journey to evolving as influencers.

I connected to the frustration that bubbled inside me and it made me want to shout, 'Can't you see that I'm not a *victim* of these challenges – I'm the *product* of them!' The problems, the challenges, the struggle are facilitators of my own evolution – they're the making of me: the power-filled, influential change-maker.' Why were those women *sorry* that I'd gone through this? It's as if we don't want to feel the pain that it takes to grow. We don't want to go through the experience – we want the baby but we don't want to go through the labour. We want the results, but we don't want to go through the process. Because it's uncomfortable, it challenges us and it's painful.

Here's the thing: we have to shift from victim identity to victor. A victim is a very different creature to a victor. If in our psyche we frame pressure, pain and struggle as problems and know ourselves as victims then all personal development and professional evolution work will do is help us become a more mature victim. First we must transform our sense of self – we must *know* that we're *victors*. Then, and only then, will development work *really* work – for us. We'll be developing, evolving victors.

We've got to get this – we've got to stop with the pity party and we've got to stop with the victim mentality. We're evolving Queen Influencers. We're the powerhouses who are about to change our world. We're the hope for the next generation of women leaders coming up behind us. What we've been through and what we're going through – all of it – is a gift for our becoming.

Things don't happen *to* me, they don't happen *to* us – they happen *for* me, *for* us, and our evolution as the women leaders and influential change-makers we're here to be and become. Pain and struggle and challenge are invitations to grow – they're invitations for us to see something about ourselves, to show us what needs to change, to alert us to things that need attention. They're not things to shy away from or avoid. They're crying out for a reframe.

THE MAGIC OF REFRAMING

I once coached a woman who worked in an organization with a toxic senior leadership culture. She came to me because she felt she wasn't being seen, heard or taken seriously by her superior, the CEO. She felt as if he wanted to receive the glory for the success of the organization. She was a Young Woman Influencer; she wanted to show what she was capable of and she truly cared about real outcomes.

She felt that her boss belittled her in meetings and that he wouldn't take her seriously. She felt he was dismissive and was pushing her back from her desire to showcase her success as a leader. She was experiencing what I call the pain of insignificance. We talked about reframing the situation. I explained that it wasn't blocking her from showcasing what she knew – it was actually inviting her to find new ways of expressing herself and as such, it represented development. If she could find a way to stop thinking of it as a pushback (even if it was intended as one) and see it as a platform for finding new ways to express herself, then it would help her to grow and learn.

Reframing works like magic. Clients who feel defeated by a situation realize through the reframing process that it's actually what they need to grow and to move towards what they want. It's not about what's going on out there – it's about what's going on inside. The shift is always remarkable.

The thing to remember when reframing is that whatever you're going through will always present you with one or more of the following:

- An invitation to *be* more influential – to go beyond your usual ways of working and step into a higher version of yourself.

- An opportunity to show up as the real you; to put into practice what you're learning about who you are and what you have to offer within your sphere of influence.

- A mirror in which to see yourself, especially where you're being inauthentic or out of alignment with the real, influential you.

Each of these components is essential for our ongoing evolution as influencers. Think about what you're going through right now. Resist the temptation to moan, bitch or give up your power and instead reframe it – feel it, acknowledge it, yield to it and ask yourself:

- What else is going on here that I can't yet see?

- How is this working in my favour?

- How am I growing in this?

- Where could this experience take me?

This is such a powerful way to muster the staying power and the endurance we need when leading important, meaningful change that matters.

HABIT #6

RELEVANCE BUILDING

In this chapter, we'll look at the need to build a bridge between your authentic, outcome-transforming ideas, insights, hunches and observations – especially those that are new, nuanced and born out of intuition or spiritual intelligence – and the solutions to the problems and challenges in the king's domain. How is what we Queen Influencers have to offer *relevant*, particularly when it comes to tackling issues associated with inequality that are not improving or that are not acknowledged or taken seriously by the king?

I once asked Tim Gallway, my former teacher and the author of *The Inner Game* series, to read my first book and write some blurb for the jacket. After doing so, he gave me some invaluable feedback: 'As I read your book I thought to myself, here's a woman with a message – she most certainly has something to say, and she's a teacher. But here's the thing, Dion: aside from your message, people want and need to know *how* you have come to know what you know.'

He was teaching me how to become more relevant in the hearts and minds of those people I was hoping to influence with my ideas – by using my personal story as it relates to the reader's mission to transform their world.

TOOTING YOUR OWN HORN

To me, being relevant is facing the challenge of communicating our value in the marketplace in a strong and honest way. Voicing our value is about building a bridge of relevance between what's needed and who we are, the value we bring, what we know, our wisdom, our ideas, our insights, our hunches, our solutions, our answers, our way of thinking, our skills – all the things that make us valuable in our organization, industry and field.

We can become aware of those things of value we bring to the marketplace through the processes of unmasking and radical self-awareness; but then we need to take it further by communicating our particular suitability for the role. To do that, we need to answer the question 'So what?' You're you, so what? You know that, so what? How does who you are and what you know relate to the biggest challenges in your organization, industry and field?

You must be able to tell people how *all of you* – what you know, what you bring and what you carry – is a part of the solution needed to solve the problems. In other words, you need to make yourself uniquely, authentically relevant to the problem, the mission and the ongoing objectives.

I've seen men talk with such confidence and bravado about their importance and relevance in a way that women often struggle to.

I once gave a presentation at a luncheon for senior women in the recruitment industry. There were about 20 women in the room and just two men, one of whom I noticed from the off because he was very dapper and had a larger-than-life personality. This man really made his presence felt during the meeting, and afterwards he gave me his business card and said he hoped we could keep in touch because he might have some work for me.

Later that day I wrote a post about the event on my LinkedIn profile, saying it'd been an honour to present to those women and remarking on how impressive and brilliant they were. I noticed that the man had also posted about the event, and when I read when he'd said it made me smile. His words suggested that he'd been a speaker at the event, the guest of honour even, rather than a participant who'd simply bought a ticket to attend it. He hadn't lied, but the implication was that he'd led the meeting and was proud to have made a contribution.

Wow, look at that! I thought. *This man's saying that the meeting wouldn't have been the same without him.* Of course he was right, but that was equally true of all those in the room who'd co-created that experience.

There's something about the ability to communicate with boldness and humility the value you're bringing that makes you relevant to the purpose of whatever it is you're doing. I think the humility aspect is really important. What's required is the creation of a very strong narrative about what qualifies us and sets us in a league of our own to contribute uniquely to the solving of problems, and then the ability to communicate that.

This is about building a personal brand. What I'm suggesting is that you create a brand awareness so that people know what you care about and what you're qualified to do. You tell them and then you take it further by telling them what that would mean for the bigger challenges, thus making your expertise relevant to particular issues. You create a bridge between who you are and what needs to happen in your realm of influence.

I'm thinking about the many times I've sat with people who moan about how things are going in their industry or organization. They tell me it's going the wrong way and I say, 'Have you *told* them that? Who knows this? Who knows what *you* know?'

Elle's Story

Elle was the head of training in a large communications firm, and she also sat on the board. She told me that in her opinion the training scheme designed to develop leaders within the organization was inadequate and missed the mark. It was unable to create the new breed of leader the organization required in order to meet its new mission statement: to become more client- and customer-friendly.

The company had set objectives around diversity, inclusion, unconscious bias and other lofty aspirations, but Elle realized that its leadership training, both in content and culture, wasn't conducive to such shifts and results. Instead, it was churning out the same kind of leaders who'd perpetuate the same kind of results.

So she'd created a side hustle: working in a small way with a group of women and training them to be leaders. She knew that this programme, which she'd written from her heart, was mind-blowing in its potential to create leadership shifts for her clients. She was so excited about what she was doing with these women and she was not excited about what she was doing with the communications firm.

We talked about her deep inner conflict. The firm paid her handsomely, not only in money but also in networks, and she was highly connected within it. She didn't like her role, but she loved the benefits of the work. Conversely, working with the women was very poorly paid and inconsistent; however, she knew she was making a colossal difference to the kind of leader those women would become.

We talked about what was missing from the training that the firm had spent a substantial amount of money creating, and Elle concluded it was 'spiritual intelligence'. The programme she'd developed for the women spoke to the heart and ignited spiritual as well as practical leadership growth. She recognized that spiritual development was the key because without it, leaders would have a 'robotic approach' when it came to matters of diversity and inclusion.

She told me, 'If you speak to the spirit of leaders, the kind of leaders they become can do ground-breaking, world-changing things.' Amen, sister! Of course, I was with her all the way, but her dilemma begged a question: 'Why don't you just tell your firm what you know about spiritual intelligence and why you believe it's the way they should go with their leadership development?'

I'll never forget her response, and I've heard the same words in some form many times since: 'They don't want that from me; they don't want to know about it. It doesn't fit with the culture. I'd lose favour.' She knew that she could make her best contribution to the organization if she was able to bring that part of herself.

Her strong conviction that spiritual intelligence is a key part of leadership development was an asset to the organization, but they didn't know it and she didn't feel confident enough to tell them, for fear of losing favour.

COMMUNICATING OUR RELEVANCE

What this story illustrates is that sometimes an organization or industry needs us to *tell* them how what we know can help them. It's not always obvious and sometimes it's disruptive to the status quo, but nevertheless it's imperative that you dare to stand and build this bridge between you, your intelligence and the problem. They need to know how who you are gives you something relevant to bring to the organization, industry and field.

As Queen Influencers we need to do the following:

- Communicate our relevance – despite who we are and what we look like – in order to combat inequality at its roots.

- Communicate *how* we know what we know and *why* people should listen to us, because relevance requires transparency. Relevance also requires courage: we need to shout about our relevance, even if it makes us unpopular.

- Determine our relevance in the fight against inequality, injustice and unfairness. To do this, we must first know it ourselves – in order for others to know it and in order to create a business case for our relevance before the king.

WHAT MAKES YOU RELEVANT?

Our contribution can be something we don't initially see as relevant. I had a client who was a passionate horticulturist with seriously impressive wisdom and knowledge of the Amazon rainforest. In our coaching conversations we delved deeply into her professional challenges and searched for new solutions, finally discovering what could make her uniquely relevant in her approach. It was all wrapped up in her deep understanding of the vast, densely populated biodiversity of the rainforest.

As we spoke about the complexities and conflicts that were rising up from the different and clashing personalities within her team and within the organization, my client began to see that the principles which enabled the multitude of life forms in the Amazon rainforest to not just coexist but thrive were an exciting exemplar and model she could elegantly transfer to the challenges in her professional space. She's currently developing her own signature diversity and inclusion framework based on this intelligence and this will distinguish her from her peers and make her of high relevance in her marketplace.

Our relevance can also come from things that make us feel ashamed or that challenge us. I've seen some big mistakes and messes become powerful messages, and some gruelling tests become compelling, influential testimonies. I've personally witnessed that my disfigurement, my skin colour and my faith – despite not being universally celebrated – are part of what makes me relevant to my clients.

A friend who had life-threatening cancer and thought she was going to die developed a very personal system to help herself through the recovery process; the experience shifted her priorities and values and she now brings what she learned from this near-death experience to her professional role, to challenge the way things have been in her industry. The fight of your life is often connected with what makes you most relevant. To explore your own relevance, ask yourself how what you've been through in life makes you uniquely, authentically relevant – we each need to answer this question for ourselves and then choose to make this link known to others.

There's never been a better time to showcase your ideas, insights and information, as well as your personality and your relevance, and there are so many platforms available to do so. Anyone can write a book now – self-publishing has never been easier – and podcasts, social media and blogs are all excellent ways to raise awareness of problems that concern you, to broadcast your relevance to the subject, and to position yourself as a relevant part of the solution. It's also never been easier to reach stakeholders, supporters and like-minded allies.

Building our relevance as we commit to evolving as influencers of the king can be fun, inexpensive and straightforward. I encourage you to use these platforms – not only to share your ideas but also to position yourself as a relevant contributor. So, what makes *you* uniquely relevant in your organizational mission for equality? Who are you talking to about that? Start today.

SHOWING RESPECT

Respect, that high regard and feeling of deep admiration we have for someone or something, can sometimes be hard to give. Why? Well, let's be frank, we don't always have these warm, fuzzy, loving feelings for the people we work with, do we? And we don't always feel deep and meaningful connection or have things in common with the people we serve. Nevertheless, if we're going to evolve as Queen Influencers respect *is* due, and not only due, but essential.

Years ago I enrolled on a leadership programme and found myself in the countryside working with horses! Apparently, the teacher promised, doing so would reveal much about participants' leadership styles and challenges. Although I was game I was also, truth be told, nervous about being in the presence of these imposing creatures. When I was called into the ring to work with 'Jack' I couldn't help but feel a little overwhelmed: he smelt funny, he was so big and so muscular, and his eyes seemed to bore right through to my soul – I actually felt him reading me.

The first exercise *sounded* straightforward enough: walk alongside the horse, gain his trust and then influence the pace and get him to follow my lead. Only it wasn't that way in practice. 'Start by matching his pace,' the instructor advised. 'Good, good, keep going… now pick up the pace, Dion, run!'

Somehow I was great at matching and pacing but when it came to leading the horse I just couldn't get him to follow me. I felt deflated and during the lunch break I shared this with the instructor. 'How on earth am I supposed to make that big, intimidating beast do what I want him to?' I complained. Her response has stuck with me to this day: 'You do it with respectful intention,' she said with a knowing smile. 'Respect is the key – the horse will feel that you respect him and choose to follow your lead.'

I worked and worked at getting Jack to follow my lead and when, on day two, he chose to follow me in a brisk gallop I was beside myself with glee. Later that day I reflected on the power of shifting from fear, intimidation and disconnection to respect – in that instance, not only my respect for the horse, but also respect for myself and respect for my right to lead him despite his size and power.

THE THREE RULES OF RESPECT

That lesson has impacted my life in a myriad of truly meaningful ways. And I've come to understand that if we're to evolve as influencers, it's imperative that we also evolve in our capacity to respect ourselves, others and the mission, even when it's hard to do so. The kind of influence we need to have with the king cannot happen without respect – so over the years I've developed some very simple rules that I've committed to live by.

1: EVERYONE DESERVES RESPECT

On welcoming a client to her session one day I noticed she looked tired and a tad fed up. When I asked her what was up, she told me about her teenage daughter, who was going through some sort of adolescent crisis. 'She's turning our home upside down,' she complained. 'Everyone's walking on eggshells around her because she's causing such a heavy atmosphere with her mood swings and challenging behaviour.'

'It's hard,' she admitted, holding her head in her hands. Then she perked up: 'But you know what? We know it's just a phase she's going through, so we've decided to make allowances for her and love her through whatever this is. She's a good girl really, despite this mad disruption!'

I was impressed by my client's willingness to choose this approach with her daughter, and I couldn't help but see that this compassion and respect could be a powerful and effective strategy in her work. She'd been struggling to get her boss on side to support her in making what she considered to be important changes, and in a previous session I'd been gobsmacked by the level of disrespect his management of the situation was stirring in her. 'He's a dickhead!' she'd exclaimed.

So in this session I made a suggestion: 'Perhaps your boss would benefit from some of that compassion and respect you're showing to your daughter?'

'What do you mean?' my client asked.

I tried again: 'Maybe you could choose to respect your boss where he's at, despite his challenging behaviour and poor leadership?'

I was unprepared for her reaction. 'He's an asshole!' she cried, getting to her feet, red-faced and angry. 'He shouldn't be in that role if he can't hack it. It's not fair! He doesn't deserve respect! He's crap!'

Another client, during a similar conversation, said of a colleague: 'She's a cold, heartless bitch and I doubt she's even got a pulse!' Sadly these sentiments aren't rare in marketplace leadership and over the years I've often seen this kind of disrespect and dishonour.

One of the most challenging Bible scriptures is in Luke 6:32–35, where Jesus says, 'If you only love the lovable, do you expect a pat on the back? Run-of-the-mill sinners do that. If you only help those who help you, do you expect a medal? Garden-variety sinners do that. If you only give for what you hope to get out of it, do you think that's charity? The stingiest of pawnbrokers does that. I tell you, love your enemies. Help and give without expecting a return.'

This scripture admonishes us to understand that *everyone* is worthy of love – even our enemies; even those we can't stand; even those who rub us up the wrong way, or try to hurt us or do us wrong. *Still* we're called to love them. I think the same is true of respect – I choose to believe that everyone is worthy of my respect. Of course this sometimes feels impossible, but I've been surprised by how much it can be done, most of the time, with a decision and intentionality.

Even When It's Hard to Give It

Years ago I was on the non-executive leadership track in a charity I supported on a volunteer basis. Although I cared passionately about the organization's mission, I disagreed with the way things were done and how it was led. I was so critical and judgemental and even though there *was* massive room for improvement within the organization and the service users really *were* struggling as a result of system failures, I didn't yet know anything about the relationship between honour, respect, authenticity and influence.

I secured an audience with the CEO and the deputies and voiced my opinions about what needed to happen and who was doing what wrong. I wasn't lying about these issues and I don't think my passion and zeal were misplaced – I genuinely wanted to see change – but my lack of regard for that culture's ways of expressing respect and honour resulted in my becoming invisible, inaudible and disconnected there.

That hurt me in the extreme because I really didn't understand why it was such a big deal. I didn't feel I'd been disrespectful, and I knew I was right about the things that were wrong. I knew there were people within the organization who felt the same as I did about what was happening and saw the challenges too, but they wouldn't speak up. It made me angry that people would just moan and groan about the things they didn't like and do nothing about them. I felt somebody had to stand up, and I decided it would be me.

At that time, I believed that being authentic was telling people exactly what I thought about things. Now I know that without respect, that can be an epic fail. My failure to influence was due to my lack of respect towards the CEO and my blatant disregard for hierarchy and lines of authority. I'm still part of that charity today and I'd be lying if I said it doesn't affect me when I see that the favour and opportunity for influence that was once opened to me is now irreversibly closed. Even though my observations, ideas and insights were valid, they meant and mean nothing without honour and respect for the people who needed to hear me.

I hadn't set out to be disrespectful, but what this experience taught me is that unintentionally withholding honour is *still* dishonour, and failing to be intentional about respect is *still* disrespect.

Even Behind their Back

Today, it's my rule that *everyone* deserves respect – even when it's hard to give it and even behind their back. This second form of respect isn't usually instinctive; in fact, it's often counterintuitive. It triggers our biases and old invisible thinking about groups of people and archetypes, as the following story shows.

One of my fellow panellists at an event was a woman of great distinction, at least on paper, and I couldn't wait to meet her and hear what she had to say. But within minutes of the opening of her presentation she sounded 'off' to me. I couldn't put my finger on it – all I knew was that inside, I was making a silent announcement: *I don't like her.*

On the way back to our hotel, the friend who'd joined me on the trip asked me what I'd thought about the woman on the panel. 'Oh, I don't know. Something didn't sit right with me about her,'

I replied. 'Oh, gosh! I'm glad you said that because I felt the same way,' my friend exclaimed.

And that was it – we were off! We thickened the atmosphere in the car with a rant about this woman. It was a full-on attack, a tirade of dishonour, and I felt dreadful afterwards as I realized I'd been the one who'd opened up the gate to disrespectful discourse. That night in my alone time with God, I said sorry, and the next morning I let my friend know that I should never have allowed or contributed to such a judgemental, disrespectful conversation. I really, really meant it.

I've learned that if I'm going to master respect, especially where it's hard, I can't open up the gate to *disrespect*: not even a little bit. If everyone is worthy of respect, I can't gossip or speak badly about anyone. *Everyone* deserves respect and I'm going to practise giving it.

As I write these words, ebbing into my consciousness is the memory of a video I watched of Maya Angelou in conversation with Dave Chappelle. If you're unfamiliar with these names, she's a world-class US author, poet and queen activist in the civil rights movement and in her realm and he's a brilliant stand-up comedian whose humour comes from the streets and raw, real racial stereotypes. They were such an unlikely pair of conversationalists and that was the whole point: the film makers wanted to see what would happen if two people who wouldn't usually meet were put together.

I remember being blown away by the video. Maya's genuine respect for Dave moved me to tears. Despite his street-rough style and cussing lexicon, she saw only the best in him. She spoke to his greatness and fortified him with her words – not in a patronizing or demeaning way but in a mutual, equal way. Maya came alongside Dave and Dave came alongside Maya, both respecting each other as equals.

You'd imagine that Maya might find some of Dave's humour offensive and yet they had this incredible bond, this incredible exchange of ideas. Maya later said of the interview, 'He is so intelligent. I think he just doesn't want people to know. He is among the best we have. We talked and talked, and the truth is, I think we lifted each other up.' This was, for me, an elegant, beautiful, monumental exhibition of respect in action. I was touched by it in an indelible way. I realized this kind of respect could change our marketplace and change our world.

2: RESPECT YO'SELF

I'm trying to convey a little attitude here because honestly, sometimes it can seem as if self-respect is a spunky act. It's so common for us to compromise on our truest core values in order to stay on the right side of the clique, or to deny ourselves the right to say 'yes' to something we want or 'no' to something we don't want, in order to curry favour.

Judging by the response I get when I highlight this finding from my experience of working with women, I know we don't always recognize our self-disrespecting ways. The truth is that it's not always immediately obvious how we disrespect our own self in leadership, but often we do. One of the perks of working with my clients in the way I do is being granted access to secret thoughts.

It's from this place of privilege that I can say with certainty that we're often the principle source of disrespect in our leadership experience. The way we talk to ourselves would never be tolerated if it came from someone else.

I once had a client who'd repeatedly tut, roll her eyes and call herself 'stupid'. When I pointed this out she'd laugh it off as though it was harmless, but our sessions eventually showed her just how deeply self-disrespect was ingrained into her leadership. Behind it was the belief that to be a CEO worthy of respect, you shouldn't make mistakes and you should know all the answers. I'm sure you can imagine how this kind of thinking and belief system played out in her leadership style.

For this woman leader, making a commitment to respect herself, despite her learning and development needs, was the key to her growth as an influencer in her organization. She later fed back to me her learning on this issue: 'Thanks for opening my eyes to the disrespect I had for myself. I can absolutely see how impossible it was for my team to respect me when I had none for myself.'

Women of Influence, I've learned that things cannot go well with us until we learn deep honour for ourselves, until we hold in high esteem the call on our lives to lead important, meaningful change. Close your eyes and breathe in this truth: you're worthy of the highest respect, despite your mistakes, despite your weaknesses, despite the gaps in your development. Be willing to learn, be willing to make things right and remember to do the following:

• Respect the value you bring.

• Respect your values and boundaries.

- Respect the call on your life to change your world in significant ways.

- Respect your right to still be learning and evolving.

Don't just read these words – really think about them. What does it mean to respect these things about yourself? What would it look like if you truly honoured and held these things in very high regard? What would change? Influential Woman, respect is a two-way street. If you want to get it, you must give it: starting with giving it to yourself.

3: STAY MISSION-CENTRIC

We're talking about respecting others when it's hard to do so, and this is where I find rule #3 really helpful. Staying mission-centric is all about seeing the person or people you struggle to respect through the eyes of the mission. If you're the kind of woman I think you are – one who's called to create significant change, to influence the marketplace king, to tear down the giant of inequality in your realm – let's face it, that's not going to happen through any one of us individually.

System change requires partnerships and strategic alliances. We need other people's buy-in, and if we're struggling to respect those people (and let's face it, that happens), I say, focus on the mission. See that although you're being challenged by the need to stay respectful to them, those people bring something of value to the mission; it's worth the investment of your goodwill because of your respect for the mission.

In my experience, this is such an easy point to overlook: we respond to not liking someone as though something's wrong, when the truth is, we can't like or be liked by everyone. And that's okay: you don't have to be best friends with your co-labourers – you just need to be respectful of the truth that teamwork makes the dream work.

In all of this I've come to know it's an uphill struggle to positively influence those you disrespect, even if you disrespect them quietly or in secret. Disrespect affects the way those we want to influence respond to us – and the responsibility for this is our own.

Your Assignment Will Find You

If you choose to adopt the seven habits we've just explored, you can't help but evolve as a Queen Influencer. You'll naturally begin to grow as a voice, as someone who should be seen and heard and taken seriously. When you commit to these seven processes, when you start to function like this, your assignment – the particular way in which you'll voice your influence to the king – will present itself to you. It'll be as if your commitment sends a signal to the universe: *I'm ready for my assignment. I'm ready to influence the king.*

Dr Laura's Story

Dr Laura Stachel is a friend I met while I was planning to raise money for charity. I decided to run a leadership event on my birthday and invite high-level influencers to talk to aspiring influencers. I didn't have a charity in mind, but when I found the term 'Solar Suitcases' online it caught my attention and led me to discover the breathtaking story of Dr Laura Stachel.

Dr Laura had been an obstetrician-gynecologist, but when health issues prevented her from practising, she decided to study for a Master's degree. As part of her dissertation research she went to a rural area of Nigeria to find out why the maternal mortality rate there was so high. What she found was that women were dying from complications of childbirth, in part because the area's electricity supply was so unstable.

She reported situations in which emergency teams couldn't be summoned because the electricity was down. Midwives were struggling to deliver babies by candlelight. Nurses couldn't adequately care for patients or administer intravenous medications. Surgeons were unable to perform emergency procedures and C-sections. Critically ill patients could not receive lifesaving care.

Dr Laura revealed how one seriously ill woman had to be turned away from the hospital because there was no power. She said that as she watched the woman's family take her away, she knew it was likely that the woman would die. 'It broke my heart. I could no longer go on living my life as though I hadn't seen this.'

I could no longer go on living my life as though I hadn't seen this. Ah, those words – I live for them! I've heard this sentiment expressed so many times by the women who've invested their time in developing the seven habits, myself included. The dire situation in this part of Nigeria became Dr Laura's assignment: from that day on, she felt compelled to get involved and to influence systemic change that would save these women's lives. She's since become an avid campaigner and activist, an influencer taking a stand for maternal health – and it's beautiful to watch.

Today she provides a practical solution with 'Solar Suitcases' that she and her husband developed as a direct response to the plight of women and medical teams worldwide. Their organization, We Care Solar, install solar electric systems for maternal health care so that women no longer have to deliver their babies in darkness. She's also campaigning, informing, alerting and raising awareness. She's on a mission to beseech the king to take heed of what's happening with these women and to respond with love. One day, as we sipped tea at my home, she told me: 'I didn't find this mission, it found me.'

If you prepare yourself by cultivating the seven habits, Influential Woman, your assignment will find you too.

FINAL WORDS

*'Those who are crazy enough to think they
can change the world usually do.'*
STEVE JOBS

Recently, I went to visit an old friend, Sharon, for the first time after she'd given birth to a baby boy. She'd longed for him since she was a child, but had delayed getting pregnant until years into her adulthood in a bid to first build her career and then establish herself as a credible leader in her field.

By the time she felt ready to be a mother it took several more years to conceive, but finally Benjamin was here – seven weeks old and the apple of his mother's eye. I was taken aback by just how deeply I enjoyed cuddling Benjamin, but it was still nice to hand him back to his mummy. After Sharon put him upstairs in his cot we dived right into a soulful sisterly catch-up, chatting for hours. But suddenly, right in the middle of a sentence, Sharon sprang to her feet.

I was a tad startled and wondered what was wrong. 'Ben's awake,' she said, as she headed towards the stairs. While she was gone, I marvelled at Sharon's response: I hadn't heard Benjamin stir, but she was so attuned to his needs that his faintest cry had caught her attention.

Do *you* hear the cries of the people within *your* sphere of influence? Do you understand what they need? Do you feel compelled to respond?

ARE YOU ONE OF US?

In a LinkedIn post I posed a question to my virtual network. It was a way of checking in with people and gauging where they were at this time of intense focus on systemic inequality and, in the wake of George Floyd's murder, on racism in particular. I noted three very loud sentiments in the responses I received:

1. Don't believe the American hype! This was an isolated event and it's not representative of the progress that's been made in the rest of the world.

2. I'm shocked, and I can't believe that things are *still* this unequal. Why, in this day and age, are we having the same conversations about racism and inequality?

3. Enough is enough! I'm deeply moved by this and I care about it! I want to be part of the solution! Things *must* change!

If you're still here with me, reading this, that speaks volumes about you. I'm willing to guess that even if at the start of this literary conversation you felt the same as the first and second group of respondents to my post, now, at this point, you share the sentiments of those in the third group.

You're one of us. You're one of those crazy believers that Steve Jobs talked about. You want change and are bold enough to dare think that *you* can be part of this change through your work. You're a hope bearer. You've conceived a dream of a better, fairer, more equal and just world – not just whimsically or superficially. I'm guessing that, deep down in your professional womb, you're one of those who carries the dream. Although you may not know how, or even if, equality is actually possible, you can't shake the visceral knowing that things need to be better among us – *now*. You sense the shift needing and wanting to happen for the greater good. You know that unjust inequality, in all its forms, must die.

I dream of a world where everyone – regardless of their gender, race, colour or creed – has a fair opportunity to be, do, have, say and create what they were born to. This is a co-mission: it's going to take all of us. My strongest conviction is that this is our moment, Influential Woman, and that as we face the unprecedented uncertainties of our time and are tasked with establishing a new/next normal in marketplace operations, the stage is set and the call has been sounded for us to ascend to a whole new dimension of influence within the system we're a part of leading.

But as I've explained, what got us here – to marketplace leadership, in the room, at the table, as part of the decision-making, culture-shaping conversation – won't get us to where we can challenge this complex, powerful system, the king, to evolve in kinder, fairer, more loving ways. If we're going to influence like *this*, we must heal, we must handle our conscious and unconscious thoughts and the biases, behaviours and beliefs that hinder the path to our thrones – where we will reign as the queens who'll make a new kind of sound and make a new kind of difference and have a new kind of influence on the heart of the king.

Through the pages of this book I've shared as best I can my conviction that the way we can do this is through the cultivation of seven new and powerful habits that'll ignite our own personal evolution as women, leaders and influential change-makers. As one who's on this journey myself I can testify that if we do this right, what we're talking about here is deeply personal, not always easy and at times downright painful. It calls us to be courageous; it insists that we gain greater command of our authority and grow in genuine confidence and congruence.

But I'm learning that as we say 'yes' and give ourselves over to what happens in response to our dedication to grow, we can't help but become more of the influencer we were destined to be. The influencer that our organizations, industries and world need us to be at such a time as this – when we have a real chance to go for hard change, significant transformation; when we have a chance to make the marketplace an undeniable, indomitable force for love, justice and equality.

Repeat after me: 'I am an Influential Woman!'

AND LASTLY...

I'm all about the *woman* behind the title. You're more than your job title. You're more than the role. You're more than just a leader. You're more than just the boss. You're a WOMAN.

If you want to up your influence; if you want to be seen, heard and taken more seriously; if you want to make more difference, challenge systemic inequality and touch the heart of the king, start with *her.* Reconnect with *her.* Listen to *her.* Acknowledge *her.* Love *her.*

Find her needs, wants, desires and values. Respect *her.* The superpower in your leadership success is... *her.* Take care of *her* with the seven habits and the influence will shift by default.

RESOURCES

Below are a few of the books, websites and other media from which I've drawn so much wisdom on my ongoing journey to becoming a Queen Influencer. I recommend that you dive into them and use them to guide you on *your* onward journey in leadership and life.

BOOKS

The Spirit Level: Why Equality is Better for Everyone, Richard Wilkinson and Kate Pickett, Allen Lane, 2009

The Inner Level: How More Equal Societies Reduce Stress, Restore Sanity and Improve Everyone's Well-being, Richard Wilkinson and Kate Pickett, Penguin Books, 2020

The Co-Creative Age: The next evolutionary phase in leadership, Sally Anderson, Evolved Leadership Publishing, 2016

The Next Half The Sky: How to Change the World, Nicholas D. Kristof and Sheryl Dunn, Virago, 2010

7 Traits of Highly Successful Women on Boards: Views from the top and how to get there, Yvonne Thompson, Panoma Press, 2014

Project Heaven on Earth: The 3 simple questions that will help you change the world... easily, Martin Rutte, Livelihood, 2018

A Voice For Now: Changing the way we see ourselves as women, Anne Dickson, Piatkus, 2003

A Woman's Worth, Marianne Williamson, Ballantine Books, 1994

WEBSITES, STUDIES, PAPERS AND PODCASTS

Women Influence Community: http://womeninfluence.club

Different Women, Different Places: www.differentwomen.co.uk

Global Women 4 Wellbeing: www.gw4w.org

'Connecting the Issues that Hold Women Back: Women in the Workplace, 2019.' An annual report by McKinsey & Company and LeanIn.Org: https://leanin.org/women-in-the-workplace-2019

'Work stress: why women have it worse than men.' World Economic Forum article: www.weforum.org/agenda/2015/10/work-stress-women-have-it-worse

'Addressing Gender Folklore: Diversity in investing, or investing in diversity?' A study by The State Street Centre for Applied Research: https://cfaboston.org/docs/WomenInitiative/GenderPaper_FINAL_r071515.pdf

Women in Leadership publication: www.wilpublication.com

'The Element of Inclusion'. A podcast by Dr Jonathan Ashong-Lamptey: www.listennotes.com/podcasts/the-element-of-inclusion-dr-jonathan-ashong-k9yGuXHNSec/

'The Women in Leadership Podcast': https://womeninleadership.ie/category/podcast/

Acknowledgements

It took a village to help me birth this book. So many people, too many to mention. Some knowingly, others without really knowing they helped me flow. But there are some who were extraordinarily instrumental in the birthing of *Influential Woman* and I want to acknowledge and honour them here.

Denise Roberts, coach, sister, friend and co-labourer; you were with me from the time the book was an embryo. The truth is that this was three other books before it was this one, and Denise was with me through them all, making sense out of my ramblings and spiritual knowings before they could be understood by anyone else. I am so grateful for your time, your patience, your long suffering, your gifts and your incredible literary talent Denise, there wouldn't be any book without you!

Jennifer Manson, The Flow Writer, who came in at the 11th hour to bring this baby to birth. You are an exceptional soul, an exquisite midwife and a true Influential Woman. You were who I needed when the deadline was approaching fast, my enthusiasm had faded and the end still felt so far away. I am eternally grateful for your loving, intuitive and profoundly skilful support.

Bianca Rochelle, my baby girl, who, right before my very eyes, has come into her own kind of Influential Woman. I can't thank you enough for the hours and hours… and hours (!) of your active listening and active encouragement. Your help with granny, your willingness to call me out on the BS and, most of all, being my prayer partner through it all.

Michelle Pilley and the Hay House UK team, thank you for bringing me into the fold. I know I'm not like you, I know we don't agree on some things, but you have chosen to give me your platform and amplify my voice anyway. This is how we change the world, so thank you!

David Hamilton, my mentor, for your kindness, foresight, direction and skilful butt-kicking. It's why I've become a published Hay House author and I will be eternally grateful to you, special man.

Then there are my inner circle people who waited patiently at the finish line, cheering loudly and calling me on to completion. When I felt like giving up, these cheers compelled me to continue. Clementina Johnson – mum; Keith Johnson – dad; Denise Johnson – sister; Brooke Johnson – niece; Hazel Ann Johnson – grandmother; Cecile Watson and Emma Clune – friends.

Frederick Augustus Martin – dad; Ruby Jones – aunt, Lydia Adina Johnson – grandmother; I hear the three of you cheering from heaven too!

Ultimately it is God I thank for placing me at the heart of such an awesome village of greatness.

ABOUT THE AUTHOR

Vongai Makamure

Dion Johnson is the Womanologist, a multi-award winning women's champion with diversity, inclusion, and authentic feminine influence at the heart of her work. As an international strategic ally and master coach to women in senior leadership, her mission is the repowerment of womanity in marketplace leadership.

Dion's clients are chief executives, directors, and heads of departments across industries because she knows that when these women truly thrive, so do boards, organizations, industries, and, ultimately, our world. Dion is challenging and changing inner narratives about what it means to be a credible influencer in today's fast-changing work space.

in dion-johnson-the-womanologist

f TheWomanologist

You Tube Dion Johnson: The WOMANologist

www.thewomanologist.com

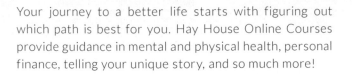

Hay House Podcasts
Bring Fresh, Free Inspiration Each Week!

HAY HOUSE

Look within

Join the conversation about latest products,
events, exclusive offers and more.

 Hay House

 @HayHouseUK

 @hayhouseuk

♥ healyourlife.com

We'd love to hear from you!